D0246588

THE ALEXANDER SHAKESPEARE

General Editor

R. B. KENNEDY

THE ALEXANDER SHAKESPEARE

King Richard III

Edited by

M. D. TAGGART

COLLINS PUBLISHERS: LONDON AND GLASGOW

First edition, 1973

0 00 325248 5
Printed in Great Britain
Collins Clear-Type Press

PREFATORY NOTE

This series of Shakespeare's plays uses the full Alexander text which is recommended by many Examining Boards. By keeping in mind the fact that the language has changed considerably in four hundred years, as have customs, jokes, and stage conventions, the editors have aimed at helping the modern reader – whether English is his mother tongue or not – to grasp the full significance of these plays. The Notes, intended primarily for examination candidates, are presented in a simple, direct style. The needs of those unfamiliar with British culture have been specially considered.

Since quiet study of the printed word is unlikely to bring fully to life plays that were written directly for the public theatre, attention has been drawn to dramatic effects which are important in performance. The editors see Shakespeare's plays as living works of art which can be enjoyed today on stage, film and television in many parts of the world.

Contents

An Elizabethan playhouse. Note the apron stage protruding into the auditorium, the space below it, the inner room at the rear of the stage, the gallery above the inner stage, the canopy over the main stage, and the absence of a roof over the audience.

THE THEATRE IN SHAKESPEARE'S DAY

On the face of it, the conditions in the Elizabethan theatre were not such as to encourage great writers. The public playhouse itself was not very different from an ordinary inn-yard; it was open to the weather; among the spectators there were often louts, pickpockets and prostitutes; some of the actors played up to the rowdy elements in the audience by inserting their own jokes into the authors' lines, while others spoke their words loudly but unfeelingly; the presentation was often rough and noisy, with fireworks to represent storms and battles, and a table and a few chairs to represent a tavern; there were no actresses, so boys took the parts of women, even such subtle and mature ones as Cleopatra and Lady Macbeth; there was rarely any scenery at all in the modern sense. In fact, a quick inspection of the English theatre in the reign of Elizabeth I by a time-traveller from the twentieth century might well produce only one positive reaction: the costumes were often elaborate and beautiful.

Shakespeare himself makes frequent comments in his plays about the limitations of the playhouse and the actors of his time, often apologizing for them. At the beginning of *Henry V* the Prologue refers to the stage as 'this unworthy scaffold' and to the theatre building (the Globe, probably) as 'this wooden O', and emphasizes the urgent need for imagination in making up for all the deficiencies of presentation. In introducing Act IV the Chorus goes so far as to say:

> '. . . we shall much disgrace
> With four or five most vile and ragged foils,
> Right ill-dispos'd in brawl ridiculous,
> The name of Agincourt.' (lines 49–52)

In *A Midsummer Night's Dream* (Act V, Scene i) he seems to dismiss actors with the words:

> 'The best in this kind are but shadows.'

Yet Elizabeth's theatre, with all its faults, stimulated dramatists to a variety of achievement that has never been equalled and, in Shakespeare, produced one of the greatest writers in history. In spite of all his grumbles he seems to have been fascinated by the challenge that it presented him with. It is necessary to re-examine his theatre carefully in order to understand how he was able to achieve so much with the materials he chose to use. What sort of place was the Elizabethan playhouse in reality? What sort of people were these criticized actors? And what sort of audiences gave them their living?

The Development of the Theatre up to Shakespeare's Time

For centuries in England noblemen had employed groups of skilled people to entertain them when required. Under Tudor rule, as England became more secure and united, actors such as these were given more freedom, and they often performed in public, while still acknowledging their 'overlords' (in the 1570s, for example, when Shakespeare was still a schoolboy at Stratford, one famous company was called 'Lord Leicester's Men'). London was rapidly becoming larger and more important in the second half of the sixteenth century, and many of the companies of actors took the opportunities offered to establish themselves at inns on the main roads leading to the City (for example, the Boar's Head in Whitechapel and the Tabard in Southwark) or in the City itself. These groups of actors would come to an agreement with the inn-keeper which would give them the use of the yard for their performances after people had eaten and drunk well in the middle of the day. Before long, some inns were taken over completely by companies of players and thus became the first public theatres. In 1574 the officials of the City of London issued an order which shows clearly that these theatres were both popular and also offensive to some respectable people, because the order complains about 'the inordinate haunting of great multitudes of people, specially youth, to plays, interludes and shows; namely occasion of frays and quarrels, evil practices of incontinency in great inns . . .' There is evidence that, on public holidays, the theatres on the banks of the Thames were crowded with noisy apprentices and tradesmen, but it would be wrong to think that audiences were always undiscriminating and loud-mouthed. In spite of the disapproval of Puritans and the more staid members of society, by the 1590s, when Shakespeare's plays were beginning to be performed, audiences consisted of a good cross-section of English society, nobility as well as workers, intellectuals as well as simple people out for a laugh; also (and in this respect English theatres were unique in Europe), it was quite normal for respectable women to attend plays. So Shakespeare had to write plays which would appeal to people of widely different kinds. He had to provide 'something for everyone' but at the same time to take care to unify the material so that it would not seem to fall into separate pieces as they watched it. A speech like that of the drunken porter in *Macbeth* could provide the 'groundlings' with a belly-laugh, but also held a deeper significance for those who could appreciate it. The audience he wrote for was one of a number of apparent drawbacks which Shakespeare was able to turn to his and our advantage.

Shakespeare's Actors

Nor were all the actors of the time mere 'rogues, vagabonds and sturdy beggars' as some were described in a Statute of 1572. It is true that many of them had a hard life and earned very little money, but leading actors could become partners in the ownership of the theatres in which they acted: Shakespeare was a shareholder in the Globe and the Blackfriars theatres when he was an actor as well as a playwright. In any case, the attacks made on Elizabethan actors were usually directed at their morals and not at their acting ability; it is clear that many of them must have been good at their trade if they were able to interpret complex works like the great tragedies in such a way as to attract enthusiastic audiences. Undoubtedly some of the boys took the women's parts with skill and confidence, since a man called Coryate, visiting Venice in 1611, expressed surprise that women could act as well as they: 'I saw women act, a thing that I never saw before . . . and they performed it with as good a grace, action, gesture . . . as ever I saw any masculine actor.' The quality of most of the actors who first presented Shakespeare's plays is probably accurately summed up by Fynes Moryson, who wrote, '. . . as there be, in my opinion, more plays in London than in all the parts of the world I have seen, so do these players or comedians excel all other in the world.'

The Structure of the Public Theatre

Although the 'purpose-built' theatres were based on the inn-yards which had been used for play-acting, most of them were circular. The walls contained galleries on three storeys from which the wealthier patrons watched; they must have been something like the 'boxes' in a modern theatre, except that they held much larger numbers – as many as 1500. The 'groundlings' stood on the floor of the building, facing a raised stage which projected from the 'stage-wall', the main features of which were:

1. a small room opening on to the back of the main stage and on the same level as it (rear stage);
2. a gallery above this inner stage (upper stage);
3. a canopy projecting from above the gallery over the main stage, to protect the actors from the weather (the 700 or 800 members of the audience who occupied the yard, or 'pit' as we call it today, had the sky above them).

In addition to these features there were dressing-rooms behind the stage and a space underneath it from which entrances could be made through trap-doors. All the acting areas – main stage, rear stage, upper stage and under stage – could be entered by actors directly from their dressing-rooms, and all of them were used in productions of Shakespeare's plays. For example, the inner stage, an almost cave-like structure, would have been where Ferdinand and Miranda are 'discovered' playing chess in the last act of *The Tempest*, while the upper stage was certainly the balcony from which Romeo climbs down in Act III of *Romeo and Juliet*.

It can be seen that such a building, simple but adaptable, was not really unsuited to the presentation of plays like Shakespeare's. On the contrary, its simplicity guaranteed the minimum of distraction, while its shape and construction must have produced a sense of involvement on the part of the audience that modern producers would envy.

Other Resources of the Elizabethan Theatre

Although there were few attempts at scenery in the public theatre (painted backcloths were occasionally used in court performances), Shakespeare and his fellow playwrights were able to make use of a fair variety of 'properties'; lists of such articles have survived: they include beds, tables, thrones, and also trees, walls, a gallows, a Trojan horse and a 'Mouth of Hell'; in a list of properties belonging to the manager, Philip Henslowe, the curious item 'two mossy banks' appears. Possibly one of them was used for the

'bank whereon the wild thyme blows,
Where oxlips and the nodding violet grows'

in *A Midsummer Night's Dream* (Act II, Scene i). Once again, imagination must have been required of the audience.

Costumes were the one aspect of stage production in which trouble and expense were hardly ever spared to obtain a magnificent effect. Only occasionally did they attempt any historical accuracy (almost all Elizabethan productions were what we should call 'modern-dress' ones), but they were appropriate to the characters who wore them: kings were seen to be kings and beggars were similarly unmistakable. It is an odd fact that there was usually no attempt at illusion in the costuming: if a costume *looked* fine and rich it probably *was*. Indeed, some of the costumes were almost unbelievably expensive. Henslowe lent his company £19 to buy a cloak, and the Alleyn brothers, well-known actors, gave £20 for a 'black velvet cloak, with sleeves embroidered all with silver and gold, lined with black satin striped with gold'.

With the one exception of the costumes, the 'machinery' of the playhouse was economical and uncomplicated rather than crude and rough, as we can see from this second and more leisurely look at it. This meant that playwrights were stimulated to produce the imaginative effects that they wanted from the language that they used. In the case of a really great writer like Shakespeare, when he had learned his trade in the theatre as an actor, it seems that he received quite enough assistance of a mechanical and structural kind without having irksome restrictions and conventions imposed on him; it is interesting to try to guess what he would have done with the highly complex apparatus of a modern television studio. We can see when we look back to his time that he used his instrument, the Elizabethan theatre, to the full, but placed his ultimate reliance on the communication between his imagination and that of his audience through the medium of words. It is, above all, his rich and wonderful use of language that must have made play-going at that time a memorable experience for people of widely different kinds. Fortunately, the deep satisfaction of appreciating and enjoying Shakespeare's work can be ours also, if we are willing to overcome the language difficulty produced by the passing of time.

SHAKESPEARE'S LIFE AND TIMES

Very little indeed is known about Shakespeare's private life: the facts included here are almost the only indisputable ones. The dates of Shakespeare's plays are those on which they were first produced.

* * *

1558	Queen Elizabeth crowned.	
1561	Francis Bacon born.	
1564	Christopher Marlowe born.	William Shakespeare born, April 23rd, baptized April 26th.
1566		Shakespeare's brother, Gilbert, born.
1567	Mary, Queen of Scots, deposed. James VI (later James I of England) crowned King of Scotland.	
1572	Ben Jonson born. Lord Leicester's Company (of players) licensed; later called Lord Strange's, then the Lord Chamberlain's, and finally (under James) The King's Men.	
1573	John Donne born.	
1574	The Common Council of London directs that all plays and playhouses in London must be licensed.	
1576	James Burbage builds the first public playhouse, The Theatre, at Shoreditch, outside the walls of the City.	
1577	Francis Drake begins his voyage round the world (completed 1580). Holinshed's *Chronicles of England, Scotland and Ireland* published (which Shakespeare later used extensively).	
1582		Shakespeare married to Anne Hathaway.

1583	The Queen's Company founded by royal warrant.	Shakespeare's daughter, Susanna, born.
1585		Shakespeare's twins, Hamnet and Judith, born.
1586	Sir Philip Sidney, the Elizabethan ideal 'Christian knight', poet, patron, soldier, killed at Zutphen in the Low Countries.	
1587	Mary, Queen of Scots, beheaded. Marlowe's *Tamburlaine* (*Part I*) first staged.	
1588	Defeat of the Spanish Armada. Marlowe's *Tamburlaine* (*Part II*) first staged.	
1589	Marlowe's *Jew of Malta* and Kyd's *Spanish Tragedy* (a 'revenge tragedy' and one of the most popular plays of Elizabethan times).	
1590	Spenser's *Faerie Queene* (Books I-III) published.	
1592	Marlowe's *Doctor Faustus* and *Edward II* first staged. Witchcraft trials in Scotland. Robert Greene, a rival playwright, refers to Shakespeare as 'an upstart crow' and 'the only Shake-scene in a country'.	*Titus Andronicus* *Henry VI, Parts I, II and III* *Richard III*
1593	London theatres closed by the plague. Christopher Marlowe killed in a Deptford tavern.	*Two Gentlemen of Verona* *Comedy of Errors* *The Taming of the Shrew* *Love's Labour's Lost*
1594	Shakespeare's company becomes The Lord Chamberlain's Men.	*Romeo and Juliet*
1595	Raleigh's first expedition to Guiana. Last expedition of Drake and Hawkins (both died).	*Richard II* *A Midsummer Night's Dream*

1596	Spenser's *Faerie Queene* (Books IV-VI) published. James Burbage buys rooms at Blackfriars and begins to convert them into a theatre.	*King John* *The Merchant of Venice* Shakespeare's son Hamnet dies. Shakespeare's father is granted a coat of arms.
1597	James Burbage dies; his son Richard, a famous actor, turns the Blackfriars Theatre into a private play-house.	*Henry IV (Part I)* Shakespeare buys and redecorates New Place at Stratford.
1598	Death of Philip II of Spain.	*Henry IV (Part II)* *Much Ado About Nothing*
1599	Death of Edmund Spenser. The Globe Theatre completed at Bankside by Richard and Cuthbert Burbage.	*Henry V* *Julius Caesar* *As You Like It*
1600	Fortune Theatre built at Cripplegate. East India Company founded for the extension of English trade and influence in the East. The Children of the Chapel begin to use the hall at Blackfriars.	*Merry Wives of Windsor* *Troilus and Cressida*
1601		*Hamlet* *Twelfth Night*
1602	Sir Thomas Bodley's library opened at Oxford.	
1603	Death of Queen Elizabeth. James I comes to the throne. Shakespeare's company becomes The King's Men. Raleigh tried, condemned and sent to the Tower.	
1604	Treaty of peace with Spain.	*Measure for Measure* *Othello* *All's Well that Ends Well*
1605	The Gunpowder Plot: an attempt by a group of Catholics to blow up the Houses of Parliament.	
1606	Guy Fawkes and other plotters executed.	*Macbeth* *King Lear*

1607	Virginia, in America, colonized. A great frost in England.	*Antony and Cleopatra* *Timon of Athens* *Coriolanus* Shakespeare's daughter, Susanna, married to Dr. John Hall.
1608	The company of the Children of the Chapel Royal (who had performed at Blackfriars for ten years) is disbanded. John Milton born. Notorious pirates executed in London.	Richard Burbage leases the Blackfriars Theatre to six of his fellow actors, including Shakespeare. *Pericles, Prince of Tyre*
1609		Shakespeare's *Sonnets* published.
1610	A great drought in England.	*Cymbeline*
1611	Chapman completes his great translation of the *Iliad*, the story of Troy. Authorized Version of the Bible published.	*A Winter's Tale* *The Tempest*
1612	Webster's *The White Devil* first staged.	Shakespeare's brother, Gilbert, dies.
1613	Globe Theatre burnt down during a performance of *Henry VIII* (the firing of small cannon set fire to the thatched roof). Webster's *Duchess of Malfi* first staged.	*Henry VIII* *Two Noble Kinsmen* Shakespeare buys a house at Blackfriars.
1614	Globe Theatre rebuilt 'in far finer manner than before'.	
1616	Ben Jonson publishes his plays in one volume. Raleigh released from the Tower in order to prepare an expedition to the gold mines of Guiana.	Shakespeare's daughter, Judith, marries Thomas Quiney. Death of Shakespeare on his birthday, April 23rd.
1618	Raleigh returns to England and is executed on the charge for which he was imprisoned in 1603.	
1623	Publication of the Folio edition of Shakespeare's plays.	Death of Anne Shakespeare (née Hathaway).

MONEY IN SHAKESPEARE'S DAY

It is extremely difficult, if not impossible, to relate the value of money in our time to its value in another age and to compare prices of commodities today and in the past. Many items are simply not comparable on grounds of quality or serviceability.

There was a bewildering variety of coins in use in Elizabethan England. As nearly all English and European coins were gold or silver, they had intrinsic value apart from their official value. This meant that foreign coins circulated freely in England and were officially recognized, for example, the French crown (écu) worth about 30p (72 cents), and the Spanish ducat worth about 33p (79 cents). The following table shows some of the coins mentioned by Shakespeare and their relation to one another.

GOLD	*British*	*American*	SILVER	*British*	*American*
sovereign (heavy type)	£1.50	$3.60	shilling	10p	24c
sovereign (light type)	66p–£1	$1.58–$2.40	groat	1½p	4c
angel	33p–50p	79c–$1.20			
royal	50p	$1.20			
noble	33p	79c			
crown	25p	60c			

A comparison of the following prices in Shakespeare's time with the prices of the same items today will give some idea of the change in the value of money.

ITEM	PRICE		ITEM	PRICE	
	British	*American*		*British*	*American*
beef, per lb.	½p	1c	cherries (lb.)	1p	2c
mutton, leg	7½p	18c	7 oranges	1p	2c
rabbit	3½p	9c	1 lemon	1p	2c
chicken	3p	8c	cream (quart)	2½p	6c
potatoes (lb.)	10p	24c	sugar (lb.)	£1	$2.40
carrots (bnch.)	1p	2c	sack (wine) (gal.)	14p	34c
8 artichokes	4p	9c	tobacco (oz.)	25p	60c
1 cucumber	1p	2c	biscuits (lb.)	12½p	30c

INTRODUCTION

A few scraps of 'information' about Richard III are widely known: that he was deformed, that he got rid of the Princes in the Tower, and that he said 'A horse! a horse! my kingdom for a horse!' Since Laurence Olivier made a film of Shakespeare's play there is also a familiar image of a twisted, shambling but nimble figure, confiding maliciously in the audience from the screen.

The play has been a popular one for nearly 400 years, and was particularly so in Shakespeare's own time. Strange, larger-than-life characters usually arouse intense interest, and it is certainly the person of Richard himself that has kept the play on the stage: there is hardly any play, apart perhaps from *Hamlet*, that depends so much on its central figure. He is grotesquely horrible and, as usual, Shakespeare wastes no time at all in involving us. Richard, alone on the stage as the play opens, presents himself as:

Cheated of feature by dissembling nature,
Deform'd, unfinish'd, sent before my time
Into this breathing world scarce half made up,
And that so lamely and unfashionable
That dogs bark at me as I halt by them—
(Act I, Scene i, lines 19-23).

Soon afterwards he announces his determination *to prove a villain*, backing it up by telling us that he has already poisoned the king's mind against his own brother, George, Duke of Clarence. No sooner has he said the words than Clarence is brought in, under guard, on his way to imprisonment in the Tower. Richard puts on a convincing show of brotherly concern, filling George's mind with all sorts of lies about other people. A few minutes later, as the wretched George is led away, Richard reverts to his 'true' manner, saying with contempt and sarcasm:

Simple, plain Clarence, I do love thee so
That I will shortly send thy soul to heaven,
If heaven will take the present at our hands.
(Act I, Scene i, lines 118-20)

Already we know what we are in for—a startling revelation of self-confident wickedness—and already we know that we're going to enjoy it, that there is a zest and thoroughness about Richard's evil character that will compel a kind of admiration. Wholehearted wickedness does fascinate, and few characters, in history or in drama, have equalled Shakespeare's Richard in this respect. How accurate a picture it is of the real Richard is quite another matter, which will be touched on in the Summing Up. It is interesting to try to decide how close to history Shakespeare's play is, but it shouldn't betray us into judging him as a historian, which he isn't. He is a dramatist, who sets out to attract our interest and to hold it, at least for the few hours during which we sit in the theatre, and, if possible, for longer than that. It is up to everyone to decide for himself how successful *Richard III* is in this respect, but it is important to see the play, when possible, and not to assess it solely on the experience of reading it. However, reading or seeing, you are likely to enjoy it more if you carry one or two questions in the back of your mind.

It has been suggested that Richard himself makes a very early, and horrific impact. There are plenty of other features which are appalling—many of them centred on Richard, but involving, in one way or another, most of the other characters—murders, battles, wailing women, ghosts and curses among them. The Elizabethans loved 'blood and thunder' and were supplied with them in large quantities by their playwrights. Over the centuries Shakespeare has come to seem a greater dramatist than any of the others. Is there anything about the play *Richard III* which suggests a power to do any more than horrify and excite? Do we see here any deeper truths about man or society, truths which may be still relevant in our own time? We are constantly being told, in the second half of the twentieth century, that we live in an age of violence; there can be little doubt that the fifteenth century was such an age, and in that respect there must be something shared across five hundred years. Is there anything else in Shakespeare's picture of that time that speaks with clear significance to us today?

LIST OF CHARACTERS

KING EDWARD THE FOURTH

EDWARD, PRINCE OF WALES, *afterwards* KING EDWARD V RICHARD, DUKE OF YORK	*sons to the* KING
GEORGE, DUKE OF CLARENCE RICHARD, DUKE OF GLOUCESTER, *afterwards* KING RICHARD III	*brothers to the* KING

A YOUNG SON OF CLARENCE (EDWARD, *Earl of Warwick*)
HENRY, EARL OF RICHMOND, *afterwards* KING HENRY VII
CARDINAL BOURCHIER, ARCHBISHOP OF CANTERBURY
THOMAS ROTHERHAM, ARCHBISHOP OF YORK
JOHN MORTON, BISHOP OF ELY
DUKE OF BUCKINGHAM
DUKE OF NORFOLK
EARL OF SURREY, *his son*
EARL RIVERS, *brother to King Edward's Queen*
MARQUIS OF DORSET *and* LORD GREY, *her sons*
EARL OF OXFORD
LORD HASTINGS
LORD STANLEY, *called also* EARL OF DERBY
LORD LOVEL
SIR THOMAS VAUGHAN
SIR RICHARD RATCLIFF
SIR WILLIAM CATESBY
SIR JAMES TYRREL
SIR JAMES BLOUNT
SIR WALTER HERBERT
SIR ROBERT BRAKENBURY, *Lieutenant of the Tower*
SIR WILLIAM BRANDON
CHRISTOPHER URSWICK, *a priest*
LORD MAYOR OF LONDON

LIST OF CHARACTERS

SHERIFF OF WILTSHIRE
HASTINGS, *a pursuivant*
TRESSEL *and* BERKELEY, *gentlemen attending on the Lady Anne*
ELIZABETH, *Queen to King Edward IV*
MARGARET, *widow of King Henry VI*
DUCHESS OF YORK, *mother to King Edward IV, Clarence and Gloucester*
LADY ANNE, *widow of Edward Prince of Wales, son to King Henry VI; afterwards married to the Duke of Gloucester*
A YOUNG DAUGHTER OF CLARENCE (MARGARET PLANTAGENET, *Countess of Salisbury*)
Ghosts *of Richard's victims*
Lords, Gentlemen *and* Attendants; Priest, Scrivener, Page, Bishops, Aldermen, Citizens, Soldiers, Messengers, Murderers, Keeper

THE SCENE: *England*

NOTES

ACT ONE

SCENE I

An audience of Shakespeare's time expected a character speaking alone to be speaking the truth. The soliloquy that opens the play therefore establishes straight away what we are to expect of Richard: aware of his own limitations he is nevertheless determined to show himself a better man than the rest, whom it is quite clear he despises. The wry humour, that is as characteristic of him as his cynical realism and cunning, can be seen to spring from this sense of his own superiority. These first forty lines not only set the tone and theme of all that is to follow, but towards their end involve us in the first of Richard's plots.

Richard's being alone on the stage at the beginning of the play draws our attention to his solitariness and uniqueness. If in performance, the actor speaks the soliloquy with his back to the audience he adds force to the impression of isolation and insolence.

1. *Now:* i.e. after the battle of Tewkesbury which finally established Richard's brother Edward as king. He, with the help of his brothers Richard and George, finally defeated the army of the Lancastrian Henry VI, who was captured and later killed in captivity.

our: i.e. for the family of York.

2. *sun of York:* a pun. Edward IV was the son of Richard, Duke of York, and the blazing sun was the Yorkists' badge.

3. *lour'd:* frowned.

house: family.

5. Victorious generals have, since Roman times, traditionally been crowned with a wreath of laurel leaves.

6. *bruised arms:* weapons and armour hacked and damaged in battle.

7. *stern alarums:* calls to the serious business of fighting, sounded on drums and trumpets.

8. *measures:* dignified dances.

9. 'War, that had such a stern and frightening face, has now smoothed out the furrows from his forehead.'

10. *barbed steeds:* horses protected by spiked armour.

12-13. 'The soldier now plays lightheartedly in a lady's room, making love to the sound of pleasant, sensual music on the lute.' Edward IV was notorious for his affairs with women, and perhaps Richard has him in mind here.

13. *lute:* stringed musical instrument similar to a mandolin or guitar.

14. Richard, as he tells his audience below, was deformed, but despite what he says here, he seems to regard these weaknesses, which he exaggerates, as a challenge, a spur to make him succeed where he might seem bound to fail. (His brothers, the king and the Duke of Clarence, were both tall, well-built men.) The other people in the play see Richard's ugly shape as a symbol of his wickedness.

ACT ONE

SCENE I—*London. A street*

Enter RICHARD, DUKE OF GLOUCESTER, *solus*

Gloucester

Now is the winter of our discontent
Made glorious summer by this sun of York;
And all the clouds that lour'd upon our house
In the deep bosom of the ocean buried.
Now are our brows bound with victorious wreaths;
Our bruised arms hung up for monuments;
Our stern alarums chang'd to merry meetings,
Our dreadful marches to delightful measures.
Grim-visag'd war hath smooth'd his wrinkled front,
And now, instead of mounting barbed steeds
To fright the souls of fearful adversaries,
He capers nimbly in a lady's chamber
To the lascivious pleasing of a lute.
But I—that am not shap'd for sportive tricks,

15. *amorous:* i.e. one used by lovers; and one that makes the user love himself.
16. *rudely stamp'd:* roughly made.
want love's majesty: am without the dignity and splendid appearance of a lover.
17. Richard is being sarcastic about the manners of lovers: the man stalks about proudly, showing himself off, while the shameless, immodest woman walks in a provocative way.
18. Richard is too short to be thought handsome.
19. *feature:* impressive appearance.
dissembling: cheating; but also Richard is suggesting that his poor appearance hides his true greatness.
20-1. Richard was born prematurely and he attributes his deformities to this fact.
21. *scarce half made up:* not properly finished. The comparison with badly-made clothes continues in line 22.
22. *unfashionable:* badly-formed, as well as different from what is considered proper.
23. *halt:* limp.
24. *piping:* Music played on pipes, for example by shepherds, is more soothing and peaceful than the warlike sound of trumpets.
26. *spy:* look slyly at.
27. *descant:* comment on; but it is another musical term, meaning to sing or play variations.
29. *fair well-spoken:* another contrast with war when speech (as well as other things) is violent and coarse.
30. A villain who admitted his villainy was a common and much-appreciated character in Elizabethan plays, particularly when he took the audience into his confidence with a knowing look.
32. 'I have begun some dangerous trouble-making.'
33. Richard has bribed people to prophesy when apparently drunk, or to tell false stories about dreams they have had, that Clarence wishes to depose the king.
libels: lies that harm someone.
38. *mew'd up:* imprisoned (an image from falconry).
39. *G:* Perhaps Richard makes it clear by the way he says this that he means to see that G for George (Clarence) will be suspected, even if he himself (G for Gloucester) is in reality a greater danger.

42. Richard's pretended ignorance of Clarence's troubles is typical of his method. The more outrageous Richard's pretence, the more we are, despite his wickedness, amused by it.

43-5. Clarence here speaks bitterly; and also (particularly) in line 46.

44. *tend'ring:* being concerned about.

45. *th' Tower:* The Tower of London; a fortress and often a prison for traitors.

Nor made to court an amorous looking-glass—
I—that am rudely stamp'd, and want love's majesty
To strut before a wanton ambling nymph—
I—that am curtail'd of this fair proportion,
Cheated of feature by dissembling nature,
Deform'd, unfinish'd, sent before my time
Into this breathing world scarce half made up,
And that so lamely and unfashionable
That dogs bark at me as I halt by them—
Why, I, in this weak piping time of peace,
Have no delight to pass away the time,
Unless to spy my shadow in the sun
And descant on mine own deformity.
And therefore, since I cannot prove a lover
To entertain these fair well-spoken days,
I am determined to prove a villain
And hate the idle pleasures of these days.
Plots have I laid, inductions dangerous,
By drunken prophecies, libels, and dreams,
To set my brother Clarence and the King
In deadly hate the one against the other;
And if King Edward be as true and just
As I am subtle, false, and treacherous,
This day should Clarence closely be mew'd up—
About a prophecy which says that G
Of Edward's heirs the murderer shall be.
Dive, thoughts, down to my soul. Here Clarence comes.

Enter CLARENCE, *guarded, and* BRAKENBURY

Brother, good day. What means this armed guard
That waits upon your Grace?

Clarence His Majesty,
Tend'ring my person's safety, hath appointed
This conduct to convey me to th' Tower.

Gloucester
Upon what cause?

Clarence Because my name is George.

53. *as I can learn:* as far as I can tell.

55. *cross-row:* alphabet, so called because in old children's primers and schoolbooks it was preceded by a cross—Christ's cross.

57. *issue:* children.

58. *for:* because.

60. *toys:* foolish, fanciful ideas.

62-70. Richard diverts any suspicion away from himself. The king's marriage to Lady Elizabeth Grey, a widow, was very unpopular (though not necessarily so with Richard who probably uses her unpopularity for his own purposes). Her family was of comparatively humble status, and many people resented their influence and increased importance when she became queen.

65. 'That makes him go to such extreme lengths.'

66. *good man of worship:* This, as in 'His Worship the Mayor', is used as a respectful form of address.

72. *night-walking heralds:* Clarence here shows his contempt for the king's servants carrying love-messages.

73. Mistress Shore was the king's mistress. The 'Mistress' here, though, is only the full form of the modern 'Mrs'.

75. *for her delivery:* for her to deliver him (i.e. to have him released). One version of Shakespeare's text reads 'for his delivery', which is more easily comprehensible to modern readers.

76. *deity:* She is a goddess in the king's eyes.

77. *Lord Chamberlain:* Lord Hastings.

78-80. *I think . . . her livery:* What we ought to do, if we wish the king to continue to think well of us, is to be Mistress Shore's servants and wear their uniform.

Gloucester

Alack, my lord, that fault is none of yours:
He should, for that, commit your godfathers.
O, belike his Majesty hath some intent
That you should be new-christen'd in the Tower.
But what's the matter, Clarence? May I know?

Clarence

Yea, Richard, when I know; for I protest
As yet I do not; but, as I can learn,
He hearkens after prophecies and dreams,
And from the cross-row plucks the letter G,
And says a wizard told him that by G
His issue disinherited should be;
And, for my name of George begins with G,
It follows in his thought that I am he.
These, as I learn, and such like toys as these
Hath mov'd his Highness to commit me now.

Gloucester

Why, this it is when men are rul'd by women:
'Tis not the King that sends you to the Tower;
My Lady Grey his wife, Clarence, 'tis she
That tempers him to this extremity.
Was it not she and that good man of worship,
Antony Woodville, her brother there,
That made him send Lord Hastings to the Tower,
From whence this present day he is delivered?
We are not safe, Clarence; we are not safe.

Clarence

By heaven, I think there is no man is secure
But the Queen's kindred, and night-walking heralds
That trudge betwixt the King and Mistress Shore.
Heard you not what an humble suppliant
Lord Hastings was, for her delivery?

Gloucester

Humbly complaining to her deity
Got my Lord Chamberlain his liberty.
I'll tell you what—I think it is our way,

81. *jealous:* suspicious—probably of Richard.
o'er-worn: worn out.
widow: the queen, who was a widow when Edward married her.
82. *dubb'd them gentlewomen:* created them gentlewomen, and so raised them in the world. This is particularly unkind to the queen who was, even before her marriage to the king, of higher social standing than Mistress Shore.
83. *gossips:* intimate friends.
85. *straitly given in charge:* strictly ordered.
87. *of what degree soever:* i.e. no-one may communicate with him in any way.

88-102. Richard with his sarcasm taunts Brakenbury, who is made very uncomfortable by Richard's ambiguous remarks.

94. *passing:* extremely.

95. *kindred:* relatives.

97. Brakenbury tries to keep himself out of trouble, but Richard's cunning fluency confuses him. Even his strong denial does not help him.

99-100. 'with one exception, whoever does wickedness with her (i.e. has sexual intercourse with her) had better keep quiet about it.'

101. Brakenbury is trapped into showing that he knows of the affair. Richard gets satisfaction from manipulating everyone, even so unimportant a person as Brakenbury.

102. *betray:* trick.

103. *withal:* in addition.

104. *forbear your conference:* refrain from talking.

106. *abjects:* most servile subjects. Brakenbury would expect instead a reference to their being the king's *sub*jects.

If we will keep in favour with the King,
To be her men and wear her livery:
The jealous o'er-worn widow, and herself,
Since that our brother dubb'd them gentlewomen,
Are mighty gossips in our monarchy.

Brakenbury

I beseech your Graces both to pardon me:
His Majesty hath straitly given in charge
That no man shall have private conference,
Of what degree soever, with your brother.

Gloucester

Even so; an't please your worship, Brakenbury,
You may partake of any thing we say:
We speak no treason, man; we say the King
Is wise and virtuous, and his noble queen
Well struck in years, fair, and not jealous;
We say that Shore's wife hath a pretty foot,
A cherry lip, a bonny eye, a passing pleasing tongue;
And that the Queen's kindred are made gentlefolks.
How say you, sir? Can you deny all this?

Brakenbury

With this, my lord, myself have nought to do.

Gloucester

Nought to do with Mistress Shore! I tell thee, fellow,
He that doth naught with her, excepting one,
Were best to do it secretly alone.

Brakenbury

What one, my lord?

Gloucester

Her husband, knave! Wouldst thou betray me?

Brakenbury

I do beseech your Grace to pardon me, and withal
Forbear your conference with the noble Duke.

Clarence

We know thy charge, Brakenbury, and will obey.

Gloucester

We are the Queen's abjects and must obey.

109. *widow:* of Sir John Grey. Richard's real or pretended dislike of the queen is summed up here.
110. *enfranchise you:* set you free.
111-16. Richard ends his conversation with Clarence with malicious humour.
111. Richard, because he is his brother, shares Clarence's disgrace.
112. *Touches me:* concerns me. A double meaning: (1) it affects me; (2) I have a part in it.
113. Clarence appears not quite sure of the genuineness of Richard's feelings.
115. *deliver:* set free from prison (one way or another).
lie: a double meaning: (1) lie in prison for; (2) tell lies about.
116. *perforce:* of necessity.

118-20. It is one of Richard's frequent jokes to say wicked things in humble, moral tones.
118. *plain:* straightforward, uncomplicated.
120. *at our hands:* offered by me.
121. *new-delivered:* recently released from prison.

125. *brook'd:* put up with.

127-8. Richard (lines 66-8) has blamed the queen's family for Hastings' imprisonment.

131. *prevail'd:* got their way with.

Brother, farewell; I will unto the King;
And whatsoe'er you will employ me in—
Were it to call King Edward's widow sister—
I will perform it to enfranchise you.
Meantime, this deep disgrace in brotherhood
Touches me deeper than you can imagine.

Clarence
I know it pleaseth neither of us well.

Gloucester
Well, your imprisonment shall not be long;
I will deliver you, or else lie for you.
Meantime, have patience.

Clarence I must perforce. Farewell.

Exeunt CLARENCE, BRAKENBURY, *and* GUARD

Gloucester
Go tread the path that thou shalt ne'er return.
Simple, plain Clarence, I do love thee so
That I will shortly send thy soul to heaven,
If heaven will take the present at our hands.
But who comes here? The new-delivered Hastings?

Enter LORD HASTINGS

Hastings
Good time of day unto my gracious lord!

Gloucester
As much unto my good Lord Chamberlain!
Well are you welcome to the open air.
How hath your lordship brook'd imprisonment?

Hastings
With patience, noble lord, as prisoners must;
But I shall live, my lord, to give them thanks
That were the cause of my imprisonment.

Gloucester
No doubt, no doubt; and so shall Clarence too;
For they that were your enemies are his,
And have prevail'd as much on him as you.

132-3. Hastings compares the royal duke Clarence with the king of birds, the eagle; while the queen's family are compared with birds of prey, the kite and buzzard, that take their chance to attack their victims while the regal bird of prey is helpless.

136. *melancholy:* depressed.

137. *fear him:* are afraid he will die.

139. *diet:* way of life.

140. 'And worn himself out.'

145-62. Richard, in outlining more of his plans, shows the energetic practical sense that leaves no room for a conventional morality, that is summed up in *bustle* (line 152), which here means to be vigorously active. His feeling that he is superior to others is implied by his attitude to his brothers.

146. *pack'd with posthorse:* sent with greatest speed.

147. *urge his hatred more to Clarence:* convince him that he ought to hate Clarence more.

148. *steel'd:* strengthened.

153. *Warwick's youngest daughter:* Lady Anne, widow of Edward, Henry VI's son. The Earl of Warwick had been an immensely powerful nobleman who had fought for both the houses of York and Lancaster.

154. *her father:* her father-in-law, Henry VI.

159. Marrying Lady Anne is a necessary step to something else Richard has in mind.

160. *yet . . . market:* I'm counting on the results of my schemes too soon.

Hastings

More pity that the eagles should be mew'd
Whiles kites and buzzards prey at liberty.

Gloucester

What news abroad?

Hastings

No news so bad abroad as this at home:
The King is sickly, weak, and melancholy,
And his physicians fear him mightily.

Gloucester

Now, by Saint John, that news is bad indeed.
O, he hath kept an evil diet long
And overmuch consum'd his royal person!
'Tis very grievous to be thought upon.
Where is he? In his bed?

Hastings

He is.

Gloucester

Go you before, and I will follow you.

Exit HASTINGS

He cannot live, I hope, and must not die
Till George be pack'd with posthorse up to heaven.
I'll in to urge his hatred more to Clarence
With lies well steel'd with weighty arguments;
And, if I fail not in my deep intent,
Clarence hath not another day to live;
Which done, God take King Edward to his mercy,
And leave the world for me to bustle in!
For then I'll marry Warwick's youngest daughter.
What though I kill'd her husband and her father?
The readiest way to make the wench amends
Is to become her husband and her father;
The which will I—not all so much for love
As for another secret close intent
By marrying her which I must reach unto.
But yet I run before my horse to market.

SCENE II

The scene begins with the first of the many curses that are laid on Richard. The Prince of Wales (eldest son of the monarch) was killed on the battlefield of Tewkesbury, and now his widow curses Richard as she mourns the death of her father-in-law, King Henry VI, who, after imprisonment in the Tower of London, has been killed so that the Lancastrian supporters will not have a claimant to the throne. As with so many of the curses and oaths spoken in the play, the fulfilment is not what Anne intends it to be. The curses must be understood to be more than a release of anger: they are believed in.

There is great intensity in the meeting of Richard and Anne. He, after asserting his authority, is full of assurance; in making his proposal of marriage to her he never appears to doubt that he will succeed: that is why he continues to ignore the curses and the withering things she says of him. Finally like an animal that has been baited (tormented) and worn itself out with attempting to fight back, Anne submits to him. Richard's comment after she has left him suggests that he was not as confident of success as he appeared to be; that part of the reason for his trying to persuade Anne to marry him was to see whether he could manage to do the seemingly impossible. Having done it, he has once again shown his superiority to others.

Stage Direction. *Halberds:* men carrying halberds, weapons like spears with battle-axe heads fixed to them.

2. *shrouded:* A shroud is a cloth covering a dead body.

hearse: a carriage for a dead body on its way to burial.

3. *obsequiously:* in a way suitable for a funeral.

4. *virtuous Lancaster:* Henry VI had been a member of the house of Lancaster. He had been noted for his religious life.

6. As ashes are the remains of burnt things, so Henry's corpse is the remains of a dynasty. *Pale ashes* are those that have long been cold and are far removed from the colour of wood, say, or flame. Henry is pale because he is dead.

8. *invocate:* call upon. She is appealing to Henry as though he were already a saint.

11. She assumes that Richard is responsible for killing both Henry and Edward.

12. *these windows . . . life:* the wounds. Windows were opened to allow the soul of a dead person to pass through on its way to heaven.

13. *balm:* soothing ointment, i.e. her tears.

16. *the blood:* the family (of him who killed Henry).

17. 'May more dreadful misfortune happen to that wretch whom all hate.'

19. Anne refers to creatures that were all supposed to be poisonous, and to cause disgust.

21. *abortive:* like a monster.

22. *prodigious:* abnormal.

untimely brought to light: born prematurely.

25. *unhappiness:* unnatural appearance and behaviour.

Clarence still breathes; Edward still lives and reigns;
When they are gone, then must I count my gains.

Exit

SCENE II—*London. Another street*

Enter the corpse of KING HENRY THE SIXTH *with* HALBERDS *to guard it;* LADY ANNE *being the mourner, attended by* TRESSEL *and* BERKELEY

Anne

Set down, set down your honourable load—
If honour may be shrouded in a hearse;
Whilst I awhile obsequiously lament
Th' untimely fall of virtuous Lancaster.
Poor key-cold figure of a holy king!
Pale ashes of the house of Lancaster!
Thou bloodless remnant of that royal blood!
Be it lawful that I invocate thy ghost
To hear the lamentations of poor Anne,
Wife to thy Edward, to thy slaughtered son,
Stabb'd by the self-same hand that made these wounds.
Lo, in these windows that let forth thy life
I pour the helpless balm of my poor eyes.
O, cursed be the hand that made these holes!
Cursed the heart that had the heart to do it!
Cursed the blood that let this blood from hence!
More direful hap betide that hated wretch
That makes us wretched by the death of thee
Than I can wish to adders, spiders, toads,
Or any creeping venom'd thing that lives!
If ever he have child, abortive be it,
Prodigious, and untimely brought to light,
Whose ugly and unnatural aspect
May fright the hopeful mother at the view,
And that be heir to his unhappiness!

26-8. The intended meaning would seem to be that Richard's wife, whoever she might be, should be made as unhappy by his *life* (not death) as the Lady Anne is made unhappy by the deaths of her husband and her king. (See Act IV, Scene i, lines 75-6.) The word 'death' does not make sense, because a wife would be most likely to be happy at the death of such an appalling husband. This mistake was probably made by actors.
29. She speaks to the Bearers.
Chertsey: the abbey at Chertsey in Surrey.
30. *Paul's:* old St. Paul's Cathedral, in London.
interred: buried.
32. *corse:* corpse, dead body.
Stage Direction. If the scene has followed without a break from Scene I, Richard can be assumed to have overheard Lady Anne's tirade, and she can be assumed now to realize that he probably has overheard her. This will give even greater sharpness to their coming encounter.

34. *fiend:* devil. Anne refuses to accept that Richard is human.
35. *charitable deeds:* acts done out of love.

36. *villains:* He calls them this because they do not obey him.

39-42. We have a glimpse of the hard and ruthless Richard here.

42. *spurn upon:* trample on.

43. Anne is horrified by Richard but is beyond fear of him.

46. *Avaunt:* Out of my way!

49. *Sweet saint:* This completes the first of the opposites that Richard and Anne use in their quarrel: he is a devil, she, a saint.
curst: spiteful.

If ever he have wife, let her be made
More miserable by the death of him
Than I am made by my young lord and thee!
Come, now towards Chertsey with your holy load,
Taken from Paul's to be interred there;
And still as you are weary of this weight
Rest you, whiles I lament King Henry's corse.

The BEARERS *take up the coffin*

Enter GLOUCESTER

Gloucester
Stay, you that bear the corse, and set it down.

Anne
What black magician conjures up this fiend
To stop devoted charitable deeds?

Gloucester
Villains, set down the corse; or, by Saint Paul,
I'll make a corse of him that disobeys!

First Gentleman
My lord, stand back, and let the coffin pass.

Gloucester
Unmanner'd dog! Stand thou, when I command.
Advance thy halberd higher than my breast,
Or, by Saint Paul, I'll strike thee to my foot
And spurn upon thee, beggar, for thy boldness.

The BEARERS *set down the coffin*

Anne
What, do you tremble? Are you all afraid?
Alas, I blame you not, for you are mortal,
And mortal eyes cannot endure the devil.
Avaunt, thou dreadful minister of hell!
Thou hadst but power over his mortal body,
His soul thou canst not have; therefore, be gone.

Gloucester
Sweet saint, for charity, be not so curst.

50. *hence:* go away from here.

52. *deep exclaims:* cries caused by deeply felt anger or pain.

53. *heinous:* wicked.

54. *pattern:* sample.

56. There was a belief that the wounds of a dead man bled again if his murderer came near him.

57. Do you think that Anne's fierce and scornful references to Richard's deformities hurt him? If they do, does he show that they do? Anne's equation of a foul, deformed exterior and a warped spirit reflects the general view of Richard. He is proud of his unnatural deeds, but perhaps not of his unnatural shape. Cf. his nephew's reference to his deformity at Act III, Scene i, line 131.

59. *empty . . . dwells:* Death was believed to cause the emptying of the veins.

67. *his:* Richard's.

68-9. Christian love should teach Anne to repay bad with good.

72. *none:* i.e. no pity.

75. *vouchsafe:* guarantee, promise.

77. *by circumstance:* with evidence.

78. *deffus'd:* shapeless. Both Richard and Anne show considerable skill in returning closely parallel expressions with widely different intentions.

Anne

Foul devil, for God's sake, hence and trouble us not;
For thou hast made the happy earth thy hell,
Fill'd it with cursing cries and deep exclaims.
If thou delight to view thy heinous deeds,
Behold this pattern of thy butcheries.
O, gentlemen, see, see! Dead Henry's wounds
Open their congeal'd mouths and bleed afresh.
Blush, blush, thou lump of foul deformity,
For 'tis thy presence that exhales this blood
From cold and empty veins where no blood dwells;
Thy deeds inhuman and unnatural
Provokes this deluge most unnatural.
O God, which this blood mad'st, revenge his death!
O earth, which this blood drink'st, revenge his death!
Either, heav'n, with lightning strike the murd'rer dead;
Or, earth, gape open wide and eat him quick,
As thou dost swallow up this good king's blood,
Which his hell-govern'd arm hath butchered.

Gloucester

Lady, you know no rules of charity,
Which renders good for bad, blessings for curses.

Anne

Villain, thou knowest nor law of God nor man:
No beast so fierce but knows some touch of pity.

Gloucester

But I know none, and therefore am no beast.

Anne

O wonderful, when devils tell the truth!

Gloucester

More wonderful when angels are so angry.
Vouchsafe, divine perfection of a woman,
Of these supposed crimes to give me leave
By circumstance but to acquit myself.

Anne

Vouchsafe, deffus'd infection of a man,
For these known evils but to give me leave

82. *patient leisure:* time set aside for you patiently to hear me plead my case.

84. *excuse current:* an excuse that would be accepted as genuine.

89. *say:* suppose.

92. *Edward's:* King Edward's.

94. *falchion:* sword.
smoking in: with the hot blood steaming on it.
95. *The which:* i.e. the sword.

101. Note Richard's tactics. Here he is disarmingly frank. At line 105 he is being callous, but his are sentiments a good Christian ought to agree with. At lines 107-8, he is perhaps becoming impatient with this line of argument.
102. *hedgehog:* a term of abuse used about someone who ignores other people's feelings. Richard's hunched back and the boar on his badge suggest the term to Anne.

By circumstance to accuse thy cursed self.

Gloucester

Fairer than tongue can name thee, let me have
Some patient leisure to excuse myself.

Anne

Fouler than heart can think thee, thou canst make
No excuse current but to hang thyself.

Gloucester

By such despair I should accuse myself.

Anne

And by despairing shalt thou stand excused
For doing worthy vengeance on thyself
That didst unworthy slaughter upon others.

Gloucester

Say that I slew them not?

Anne Then say they were not slain.
But dead they are, and, devilish slave, by thee.

Gloucester

I did not kill your husband.

Anne Why, then he is alive.

Gloucester

Nay, he is dead, and slain by Edward's hands.

Anne

In thy foul throat thou liest: Queen Margaret saw
Thy murd'rous falchion smoking in his blood;
The which thou once didst bend against her breast,
But that thy brothers beat aside the point.

Gloucester

I was provoked by her sland'rous tongue
That laid their guilt upon my guiltless shoulders.

Anne

Thou wast provoked by thy bloody mind,
That never dream'st on aught but butcheries.
Didst thou not kill this king?

Gloucester I grant ye.

Anne

Dost grant me, hedgehog? Then, God grant me too

107. *holp:* helped.
thither: there.

112. Anne again makes a wish that will turn against herself.

115. *keen encounter:* Their quarrel is like a fight in which the blows fall hard and quickly one after the other.
116. *something:* rather.
117. *timeless:* untimely, premature.

120. *effect:* the person who carries out an action.

121. *effect:* the result of an action.

123-4. 'So that I swore that I would kill all the inhabitants of the world so that I could be loved by you, even if only for one hour.'

Thou mayst be damned for that wicked deed!
O, he was gentle, mild, and virtuous!

Gloucester

The better for the King of Heaven, that hath him.

Anne

He is in heaven, where thou shalt never come.

Gloucester

Let him thank me that holp to send him thither,
For he was fitter for that place than earth.

Anne

And thou unfit for any place but hell.

Gloucester

Yes, one place else, if you will hear me name it.

Anne

Some dungeon.

Gloucester Your bed-chamber.

Anne

Ill rest betide the chamber where thou liest!

Gloucester

So will it, madam, till I lie with you.

Anne

I hope so.

Gloucester

I know so. But, gentle Lady Anne,
To leave this keen encounter of our wits,
And fall something into a slower method—
Is not the causer of the timeless deaths
Of these Plantagenets, Henry and Edward,
As blameful as the executioner?

Anne

Thou wast the cause and most accurs'd effect.

Gloucester

Your beauty was the cause of that effect—
Your beauty that did haunt me in my sleep
To undertake the death of all the world
So I might live one hour in your sweet bosom.

125. *homicide:* murderer.

128. 'If I were near you I would not let you spoil it.'

130. *that:* i.e. her beauty.

132. Already Anne has laid more than one curse on herself without intending to.

133. If she were the sun ('the day') and Richard's life (he means 'what makes life worth living'), she would be glad to take away both these things.

138. *bereft:* deprived.

142. *Plantagenet:* The Houses of York and Lancaster, to which Richard and Henry belonged, were branches of the same family.

144. *Where is he?* Anne, to make Richard more angry, is pretending not to understand that he means himself. She is also repeating the idea that no man could be better than her husband had been.

Anne
If I thought that, I tell thee, homicide,
These nails should rend that beauty from my cheeks.

Gloucester
These eyes could not endure that beauty's wreck;
You should not blemish it if I stood by.
As all the world is cheered by the sun,
So I by that; it is my day, my life.

Anne
Black night o'ershade thy day, and death thy life!

Gloucester
Curse not thyself, fair creature; thou art both.

Anne
I would I were, to be reveng'd on thee.

Gloucester
It is a quarrel most unnatural,
To be reveng'd on him that loveth thee.

Anne
It is a quarrel just and reasonable,
To be reveng'd on him that kill'd my husband.

Gloucester
He that bereft thee, lady, of thy husband
Did it to help thee to a better husband.

Anne
His better doth not breathe upon the earth.

Gloucester
He lives that loves thee better than he could.

Anne
Name him.

Gloucester Plantagenet.

Anne Why, that was he.

Gloucester
The self-same name, but one of better nature.

Anne
Where is he?

Gloucester
Here. [*She spits at him*] Why dost thou spit at me?

145. *mortal:* deadly.
for thy sake! that is what you deserve. Anne's spitting at Richard is the climax of her anger, her last attack on him, and it sums up her hatred and loathing of him. She seems now to be exhausted, without having been able to disturb Richard or turn him from his course. He still stands in front of her, following up his argument. He is at last, now that Anne is quiet, able to speak at length, and does so most effectively, comparing his earlier hard, cruel self with his present softened nature.
147. It was a common belief that toads were covered with poisonous slime.

150. *basilisks:* imaginary reptiles that could kill people by looking at them.

152. 'For now, although I am still alive, like a dead person I have none of the things that make life worth living.'

154. '(The beauty of your eyes) made me ashamed to look up because I wept like a child.'
155. *remorseful:* pitiful.

157. *Rutland:* another brother of Richard, killed in battle by Lord Clifford.
158. *black-fac'd:* i.e. because he was angry. Rutland's father, the Duke of York, had killed Clifford's father.

164. *My manly eyes:* Richard could not shed childish tears.

165. *exhale:* draw out.

167. *sued:* asked a favour.

168. *smoothing:* flattering.

169. 'But now that it seems possible that I shall have your beauty as my reward. . . .'

Anne

Would it were mortal poison, for thy sake!

Gloucester

Never came poison from so sweet a place.

Anne

Never hung poison on a fouler toad.
Out of my sight! Thou dost infect mine eyes.

Gloucester

Thine eyes, sweet lady, have infected mine.

Anne

Would they were basilisks to strike thee dead!

Gloucester

I would they were, that I might die at once;
For now they kill me with a living death.
Those eyes of thine from mine have drawn salt tears,
Sham'd their aspects with store of childish drops—
These eyes, which never shed remorseful tear,
No, when my father York and Edward wept
To hear the piteous moan that Rutland made
When black-fac'd Clifford shook his sword at him;
Nor when thy warlike father, like a child,
Told the sad story of my father's death,
And twenty times made pause to sob and weep
That all the standers-by had wet their cheeks
Like trees bedash'd with rain—in that sad time
My manly eyes did scorn an humble tear;
And what these sorrows could not thence exhale
Thy beauty hath, and made them blind with weeping.
I never sued to friend nor enemy;
My tongue could never learn sweet smoothing word;
But, now thy beauty is propos'd my fee,
My proud heart sues, and prompts my tongue to speak.

She looks scornfully at him

Teach not thy lip such scorn; for it was made
For kissing, lady, not for such contempt.

173-83. The risk that Anne will stab him must be a great one: after lines 179 and 181 she is about to plunge the sword in him. The excitement of running this risk must be very great for Richard. It puts to the severest test his belief that he can control and outwit anyone he chooses. Good acting can make this a moment of real tension.

181. *dispatch:* get on with killing me.
184. *dissembler:* someone who hides his true feelings.

187. Anne's answer to Richard's offer forces him to show that he is not being frank and honest.

191. *accessary:* a partner in committing a crime, but not the one chiefly responsible.

192. This is the first admission by Anne that she is not sure of herself.

193. *figur'd:* shown, drawn.

194. *false:* lying.

196. *put up:* put in its sheath.

If thy revengeful heart cannot forgive,
Lo here I lend thee this sharp-pointed sword;
Which if thou please to hide in this true breast
And let the soul forth that adoreth thee,
I lay it naked to the deadly stroke,
And humbly beg the death upon my knee.

He lays his breast open; she offers at it with his sword

Nay, do not pause; for I did kill King Henry—
But 'twas thy beauty that provoked me.
Nay, now dispatch; 'twas I that stabb'd young Edward—
But 'twas thy heavenly face that set me on.

She falls the sword

Take up the sword again, or take up me.

Anne
Arise, dissembler; though I wish thy death,
I will not be thy executioner.

Gloucester
Then bid me kill myself, and I will do it.

Anne
I have already.

Gloucester That was in thy rage.
Speak it again, and even with the word
This hand, which for thy love did kill thy love,
Shall for thy love kill a far truer love;
To both their deaths shalt thou be accessary.

Anne
I would I knew thy heart.

Gloucester
'Tis figur'd in my tongue.

Anne
I fear me both are false.

Gloucester
Then never was man true.

Anne
Well, well, put up your sword.

200. Anne means that she hopes all men live in hope of being forgiven by God.

202. 'I will take the ring, but I don't promise anything in return.'

206. *poor devoted servant:* i.e. Richard.

210. *these sad designs:* the intention of following Henry's body to its tomb.
211. Richard means himself.
212. *presently:* immediately.
repair: go.
Crosby House: Richard's London house, also called Crosby Place.

216. *with . . . duty:* carrying out my duty with the greatest haste I can.
217. *divers:* various.
unknown: secret.
beseech: beg of.
218. *boon:* favour.

Gloucester
Say, then, my peace is made.
Anne
That shalt thou know hereafter.
Gloucester
But shall I live in hope?
Anne
All men, I hope, live so.
Gloucester
Vouchsafe to wear this ring.
Anne
To take is not to give.

Puts on the ring

Gloucester
Look how my ring encompasseth thy finger,
Even so thy breast encloseth my poor heart;
Wear both of them, for both of them are thine.
And if thy poor devoted servant may
But beg one favour at thy gracious hand,
Thou dost confirm his happiness for ever.
Anne
What is it?
Gloucester
That it may please you leave these sad designs
To him that hath most cause to be a mourner,
And presently repair to Crosby House;
Where—after I have solemnly interr'd
At Chertsey monast'ry this noble king,
And wet his grave with my repentant tears—
I will with all expedient duty see you.
For divers unknown reasons, I beseech you,
Grant me this boon.
Anne
With all my heart; and much it joys me too
To see you are become so penitent.
Tressel and Berkeley, go along with me.

226. *attend:* wait for.

227-63. Lines 201-24 were gentler than anyone could have expected at the beginning of the scene, with Richard passing from rather dramatic protestations to an apparently genuine tenderness which called out a tender response in Anne. Richard himself hardly believed it possible, as the coming soliloquy shows. His outrageous triumph delights him, not because he particularly wants Anne for herself but because he has proved his own genius.

227. *humour:* mood.

230. *What!* Would you believe it!

233. *bleeding witness of my hatred by:* the body, bleeding afresh (beside them as they talked) was evidence of Richard's hatred of the whole House of Lancaster.

234. *bars:* barriers, disadvantages.

237. *all the world to nothing!* with odds of everything to nothing against me.

238. *Ha!* Eh? Perhaps he chuckles here.

243. 'Nature was generous with her gifts when she made him.' Did Richard genuinely admire Edward? Or was he really consumed with envy?

245. *afford:* show, provide.

246. *abase . . . me:* lower her gaze to look at me.

247. *cropp'd the golden prime:* cut short his life when it was at its glorious best.

249. *moiety:* half.

Gloucester
Bid me farewell.
Anne 'Tis more than you deserve;
But since you teach me how to flatter you,
Imagine I have said farewell already.

Exeunt two GENTLEMEN *with* LADY ANNE

Gloucester
Sirs, take up the corse.
Gentlemen Towards Chertsey, noble lord?
Gloucester
No, to White Friars; there attend my coming.

Exeunt all but GLOUCESTER

Was ever woman in this humour woo'd?
Was ever woman in this humour won?
I'll have her; but I will not keep her long.
What! I that kill'd her husband and his father—
To take her in her heart's extremest hate,
With curses in her mouth, tears in her eyes,
The bleeding witness of my hatred by;
Having God, her conscience, and these bars against me,
And I no friends to back my suit at all
But the plain devil and dissembling looks,
And yet to win her, all the world to nothing!
Ha!
Hath she forgot already that brave prince,
Edward, her lord, whom I, some three months since,
Stabb'd in my angry mood at Tewksbury?
A sweeter and a lovclicr gentleman—
Fram'd in the prodigality of nature,
Young, valiant, wise, and no doubt right royal—
The spacious world cannot again afford;
And will she yet abase her eyes on me,
That cropp'd the golden prime of this sweet prince
And made her widow to a woeful bed?
On me, whose all not equals Edward's moiety?

251. *denier:* a small copper coin.

256. *a score:* twenty.

SCENE III

The scene shows clearly the background of quarrelling, distrust, and oath-breaking that is the setting of Richard's ambition, and a situation that he uses skilfully to his advantage. Many of his victims are assembled in this scene; and Queen Margaret, widow of King Henry VI, is an important link with past events. For many years she had in effect been leader of the Lancastrian party, and an enemy in particular of Richard, Duke of York, father of Edward IV, Clarence and Gloucester. Her appearance now is like Fate in human form: what she has to say shows us that she did wrong and was punished; that those she addresses have done wrong and deserve to be punished; and her curses make it sure that they will be punished. Her presence in the scene makes us think of earlier events and look forward to what will come later, and in this way helps us to feel that the quarrels and tricks we are watching are part of a much bigger pattern of events, outside the control of the people we are watching.

Stage Direction. Lord Rivers is the queen's brother, and Lord Grey her son by her former marriage.

3. *brook it ill:* take it badly.

4. *entertain good comfort:* be prepared to be comforted.

5. *quick and merry eyes:* cheerful looks.

6. The queen knows that people dislike her.

8. The queen feels this, not only because she loves him, but also because if he died he could not protect her from other harm.

9. *a goodly son:* Edward, Prince of Wales, her son by Edward.

On me, that halts and am misshapen thus?
My dukedom to a beggarly denier,
I do mistake my person all this while.
Upon my life, she finds, although I cannot,
Myself to be a marv'llous proper man.
I'll be at charges for a looking-glass,
And entertain a score or two of tailors
To study fashions to adorn my body.
Since I am crept in favour with myself,
I will maintain it with some little cost.
But first I'll turn yon fellow in his grave,
And then return lamenting to my love.
Shine out, fair sun, till I have bought a glass,
That I may see my shadow as I pass.

Exit

SCENE III—*London. The palace*

Enter QUEEN ELIZABETH, LORD RIVERS, *and* LORD GREY

Rivers
Have patience, madam; there's no doubt his Majesty
Will soon recover his accustom'd health.

Grey
In that you brook it ill, it makes him worse;
Therefore, for God's sake, entertain good comfort,
And cheer his Grace with quick and merry eyes.

Queen Elizabeth
If he were dead, what would betide on me?

Grey
No other harm but loss of such a lord.

Queen Elizabeth
The loss of such a lord includes all harms.

Grey
The heavens have bless'd you with a goodly son

11-12. *his minority . . . Gloucester:* Richard of Gloucester is to be appointed Protector of the state (in effect the ruler) until the Prince of Wales reaches manhood.

15. *determin'd, not concluded:* settled, but not actually made law.

16. *miscarry:* die.

Stage Direction. Derby is often referred to as Lord Stanley, or simply Stanley, in other scenes.

20. The Countess Richmond is mentioned here to introduce early into the play, the threat that will eventually defeat Richard. The Countess is the wife of Lord Derby, but formerly was married to Edmund Tudor. Her son by him is Henry Tudor, Earl of Richmond, who will defeat Richard and reign as Henry VII.

24. *arrogance:* her pride, shown by her wanting the crown for her son.

28-9. *which I think . . . malice:* These words might be roughly paraphrased as follows: 'She has no control over her feelings; it's not that she really hates you.'

31. *But now:* at this very moment.

33. *amendment:* improvement in health.

To be your comforter when he is gone.

Queen Elizabeth

Ah, he is young; and his minority
Is put unto the trust of Richard Gloucester,
A man that loves not me, nor none of you.

Rivers

Is it concluded he shall be Protector?

Queen Elizabeth

It is determin'd, not concluded yet;
But so it must be, if the King miscarry.

Enter BUCKINGHAM *and* DERBY

Grey

Here come the Lords of Buckingham and Derby.

Buckingham

Good time of day unto your royal Grace!

Derby

God make your Majesty joyful as you have been.

Queen Elizabeth

The Countess Richmond, good my Lord of Derby,
To your good prayer will scarcely say amen.
Yet, Derby, notwithstanding she's your wife
And loves not me, be you, good lord, assur'd
I hate not you for her proud arrogance.

Derby

I do beseech you, either not believe
The envious slanders of her false accusers;
Or, if she be accus'd on true report,
Bear with her weakness, which I think proceeds
From wayward sickness and no grounded malice.

Queen Elizabeth

Saw you the King to-day, my Lord of Derby?

Derby

But now the Duke of Buckingham and I
Are come from visiting his Majesty.

Queen Elizabeth

What likelihood of his amendment, lords?

36. *make atonement:* bring them together (literally 'make them one').
37. *your brother:* Shakespeare seems to think that Lord Grey is her brother, not her son.
38. *my Lord Chamberlain:* Lord Hastings.
39. *warn:* summon.

Stage Direction. The Marquis of Dorset is the queen's other son by her earlier marriage.

42. Notice how often Richard enters with a burst of energy, on the attack. Here, by referring to stories that suggest he is trying to stir up feeling against the queen and her family, he succeeds in making everyone feel insecure and distrustful.
44. *stern:* a hard opponent.
them: the queen's relations.
46. *dissentious:* causing quarrels.
47-50. It is one of Richard's regular pretences that he is too simple to put on these acts; but while he is denying it he is, of course, using just this sort of cunning.
48. *cog:* cheat.
49. *French nods:* France had a reputation as the centre of fashionable—and affected—manners.
apish courtesy: the fashion of exaggerated 'good' manners.
50. *held:* thought to be.
rancorous: quarrelsome.
51. *plain:* simple.
53. *silken:* fancily dressed in silk. Again Richard contrasts his own plainness (and therefore—he likes to pretend—honesty) with the fashionable artificiality of the rest of the court.
sly, insinuating Jacks: low, common fellows, who spread lies and work themselves into favour.
54. Do you think that Grey really does not know, or that he is trying to confuse Richard by asking this direct question?
57. *Or thee, or thee:* Rivers and Dorset.
faction: the supporters of one side in a quarrel.
59. Richard strikes a telling blow here. If the king died, the queen's family would try to rule through the young King Edward V.
60. *scarce a breathing while:* hardly long enough for him to take a breath.

Buckingham

Madam, good hope; his Grace speaks cheerfully.

Queen Elizabeth

God grant him health! Did you confer with him?

Buckingham

Ay, madam; he desires to make atonement
Between the Duke of Gloucester and your brothers,
And between them and my Lord Chamberlain;
And sent to warn them to his royal presence.

Queen Elizabeth

Would all were well! But that will never be.
I fear our happiness is at the height.

Enter GLOUCESTER, HASTINGS, *and* DORSET

Gloucester

They do me wrong, and I will not endure it.
Who is it that complains unto the King
That I, forsooth, am stern and love them not?
By holy Paul, they love his Grace but lightly
That fill his ears with such dissentious rumours.
Because I cannot flatter and look fair,
Smile in men's faces, smooth, deceive, and cog,
Duck with French nods and apish courtesy,
I must be held a rancorous enemy.
Cannot a plain man live and think no harm
But thus his simple truth must be abus'd
With silken, sly, insinuating Jacks?

Grey

To who in all this presence speaks your Grace?

Gloucester

To thee, that hast nor honesty nor grace.
When have I injur'd thee? when done thee wrong,
Or thee, or thee, or any of your faction?
A plague upon you all! His royal Grace—
Whom God preserve better than you would wish!—
Cannot be quiet scarce a breathing while

61. *lewd:* wicked.

63. *on his . . . disposition:* from his own inclination, i.e. the king has decided for himself.

65. *aiming, belike:* probably guessing.

68. *ground:* reason, cause.

70. Richard means that everything is turned upside down; nobody knows what to think of people any more.

71. Richard is again attacking the queen and her family.

76. *I have need of you:* I am in a state of need because of you.

80. *ennoble:* make noblemen of.

81. *noble:* a gold coin said to be equivalent to about 34p.

82. *this careful height:* this important position, full of worries.

83. *hap:* life; the position in life that God had put her in.

84. *incense:* provoke, stir up.

88. *draw:* invoke.
suspects: suspicions.

89. 'You may deny that you were the cause.'

90. *late:* recent.

But you must trouble him with lewd complaints.

Queen Elizabeth

Brother of Gloucester, you mistake the matter.
The King, on his own royal disposition
And not provok'd by any suitor else—
Aiming, belike, at your interior hatred
That in your outward action shows itself
Against my children, brothers, and myself—
Makes him to send that he may learn the ground.

Gloucester

I cannot tell; the world is grown so bad
That wrens make prey where eagles dare not perch.
Since every Jack became a gentleman,
There's many a gentle person made a Jack.

Queen Elizabeth

Come, come, we know your meaning, brother Gloucester:
You envy my advancement and my friends';
God grant we never may have need of you!

Gloucester

Meantime, God grants that I have need of you.
Our brother is imprison'd by your means,
Myself disgrac'd, and the nobility
Held in contempt; while great promotions
Are daily given to ennoble those
That scarce some two days since were worth a noble.

Queen Elizabeth

By Him that rais'd me to this careful height
From that contented hap which I enjoy'd,
I never did incense his Majesty
Against the Duke of Clarence, but have been
An earnest advocate to plead for him.
My lord, you do me shameful injury
Falsely to draw me in these vile suspects.

Gloucester

You may deny that you were not the mean
Of my Lord Hastings' late imprisonment.

91. Lord Rivers wants to say, perhaps, 'she had nothing to do with it.'

92. *She may, Lord Rivers?* Richard cannot be shamed into silence or a less aggressive attitude by the reasonable argument of Lord Rivers; he is instead provoked to a more direct attack. Anyone who tries to argue with Richard may find his words twisted and used against him, as again at line 99.
94. *preferments:* promotions, appointments.
96. *high desert:* great worth (that makes you deserve them).
97. *What may she not?* In other words, she may do anything.
marry: indeed, truly.

99. *marry:* be married to someone.

100. Richard seems to admire his brother's good looks and fine appearance.
101. *Iwis:* certainly.
grandam: grandmother.

103. *upbraidings:* criticisms.

108. *baited:* taunted.

Stage Direction. Queen Margaret is not seen or heard by the other characters until line 157, but she is seen by the audience, ready to burst in.

111. 'The respect people show you, the ceremonial you enjoy, and your throne, all ought to be mine.'

112. 'Are you trying to frighten me by threatening to tell the king?'

113. *Look what:* whatever.

114. *avouch't:* stand by it, say it again.

115. *adventure:* risk.

116. *pains:* efforts in working and fighting for the king.

Rivers

She may, my lord; for—

Gloucester

She may, Lord Rivers? Why, who knows not so?
She may do more, sir, than denying that:
She may help you to many fair preferments
And then deny her aiding hand therein,
And lay those honours on your high desert.
What may she not? She may—ay, marry, may she—

Rivers

What, marry, may she?

Gloucester

What, marry, may she? Marry with a king,
A bachelor, and a handsome stripling too.
Iwis your grandam had a worser match.

Queen Elizabeth

My Lord of Gloucester, I have too long borne
Your blunt upbraidings and your bitter scoffs.
By heaven, I will acquaint his Majesty
Of those gross taunts that oft I have endur'd.
I had rather be a country servant-maid
Than a great queen with this condition—
To be so baited, scorn'd, and stormed at.

Enter old QUEEN MARGARET, *behind*

Small joy have I in being England's Queen.

Queen Margaret

And lessen'd be that small, God, I beseech Him!
Thy honour, state, and seat, is due to me.

Gloucester

What! Threat you me with telling of the King?
Tell him and spare not. Look what I have said
I will avouch't in presence of the King.
I dare adventure to be sent to th' Tow'r.
'Tis time to speak—my pains are quite forgot.

Queen Margaret

Out, devil! I do remember them too well:

122. *adversaries:* opponents.

127. *Were factions for:* were on the side of, fought for.

129. *battle:* army.

134. *his father:* his father-in-law. Warwick at one time supported the Lancastrian party, taking Clarence with him. But Clarence deserted again to go back to support his brother Edward.
135. *foreswore himself:* broke his oath.

138. *meed:* reward.

141. It is difficult to imagine whom Richard thinks he is deceiving here. The truth is, he is always acting a part.

142. *Hie:* go.

143. *cacodemon:* evil spirit.
there thy kingdom is: i.e. in hell.

Thou kill'dst my husband Henry in the Tower,
And Edward, my poor son, at Tewksbury.

Gloucester

Ere you were queen, ay, or your husband king,
I was a pack-horse in his great affairs,
A weeder-out of his proud adversaries,
A liberal rewarder of his friends;
To royalize his blood I spent mine own.

Queen Margaret

Ay, and much better blood than his or thine.

Gloucester

In all which time you and your husband Grey
Were factious for the house of Lancaster;
And, Rivers, so were you. Was not your husband
In Margaret's battle at Saint Albans slain?
Let me put in your minds, if you forget,
What you have been ere this, and what you are;
Withal, what I have been, and what I am.

Queen Margaret

A murd'rous villain, and so still thou art.

Gloucester

Poor Clarence did forsake his father, Warwick,
Ay, and forswore himself—which Jesu pardon!—

Queen Margaret

Which God revenge!

Gloucester

To fight on Edward's party for the crown;
And for his meed, poor lord, he is mewed up.
I would to God my heart were flint like Edward's,
Or Edward's soft and pitiful like mine.
I am too childish-foolish for this world.

Queen Margaret

Hie thee to hell for shame and leave this world,
Thou cacodemon; there thy kingdom is.

Rivers

My Lord of Gloucester, in those busy days
Which here you urge to prove us enemies,

148. *pedlar:* wandering salesman.

157. *pirates:* probably applied to all those who rob with violence, by sea or land.
158. *pill'd:* stolen.

160-1. 'If you don't bow before me as your queen (and tremble in your humility), yet you ought to tremble when you see me, for I am a queen whom you rebels have deposed (and your punishment will follow).'
162. *gentle villain:* There is a double sarcasm here. *Gentle* means (1) kindly and (2) well-born; *villain* means (1) peasant and (2) scoundrel. Margaret is throwing back at Richard his remarks about Queen Elizabeth and her low birth, and his own claim that he is pitiable.
163. *what mak'st thou?* what are you doing?
164. 'I have only come to recite the list of your crimes.'
marr'd: spoiled. It balances the word *make,* which Margaret takes in its ordinary sense.

168. *abode:* stay.

170. *thou:* Queen Elizabeth.

We follow'd then our lord, our sovereign king.
So should we you, if you should be our king.

Gloucester

If I should be! I had rather be a pedlar.
Far be it from my heart, the thought thereof!

Queen Elizabeth

As little joy, my lord, as you suppose
You should enjoy were you this country's king,
As little joy you may suppose in me
That I enjoy, being the Queen thereof.

Queen Margaret

As little joy enjoys the Queen thereof;
For I am she, and altogether joyless.
I can no longer hold me patient.

Advancing

Hear me, you wrangling pirates, that fall out
In sharing that which you have pill'd from me.
Which of you trembles not that looks on me?
If not that, I am Queen, you bow like subjects,
Yet that, by you depos'd, you quake like rebels?
Ah, gentle villain, do not turn away!

Gloucester

Foul wrinkled witch, what mak'st thou in my sight?

Queen Margaret

But repetition of what thou hast marr'd,
That will I make before I let thee go.

Gloucester

Wert thou not banished on pain of death?

Queen Margaret

I was; but I do find more pain in banishment
Than death can yield me here by my abode.
A husband and a son thou ow'st to me;
And thou a kingdom; all of you allegiance.
This sorrow that I have by right is yours;
And all the pleasures you usurp are mine.

173. *curse:* This is the second occasion in the play on which curses have been talked about, and the first reference to the fulfilling of a curse.
174. *crown . . . paper!* Richard, Duke of York, had claimed the throne in Henry VI's reign, but had been defeated in battle by Margaret, who mockingly crowned him with a paper crown before having him killed.
176. *clout:* cloth.
177. *steep'd in:* soaked in.
faultless: innocent.
pretty Rutland: What is the effect of 'pretty' here, and 'babe' in line 182? Rutland, though the youngest of York's sons, was not an infant.
181. *right:* avenge.

193. *Should all but answer for:* all these things together could not quit pay for.
that . . . brat: This is another view of Rutland, previously callec 'pretty babe'.
195. *quick:* vigorous, full of life.
196-233. Every curse is later fulfilled; each victim remembers the curs when it is fulfilled. Queen Margaret appears again to enjoy her trumpl in Act IV, Scene iv.
196. *surfeit:* excessive self-indulgence.
197. King Henry was murdered so that Edward IV could be secure.
199. *our son:* Margaret speaks like a queen, using the royal 'we'.

Gloucester
The curse my noble father laid on thee,
When thou didst crown his warlike brows with paper
And with thy scorns drew'st rivers from his eyes,
And then to dry them gav'st the Duke a clout
Steep'd in the faultless blood of pretty Rutland—
His curses then from bitterness of soul
Denounc'd against thee are all fall'n upon thee;
And God, not we, hath plagu'd thy bloody deed.

Queen Elizabeth
So just is God to right the innocent.

Hastings
O, 'twas the foulest deed to slay that babe,
And the most merciless that e'er was heard of!

Rivers
Tyrants themselves wept when it was reported.

Dorset
No man but prophesied revenge for it.

Buckingham
Northumberland, then present, wept to see it.

Queen Margaret
What, were you snarling all before I came,
Ready to catch each other by the throat,
And turn you all your hatred now on me?
Did York's dread curse prevail so much with heaven
That Henry's death, my lovely Edward's death,
Their kingdom's loss, my woeful banishment,
Should all but answer for that peevish brat?
Can curses pierce the clouds and enter heaven?
Why then, give way, dull clouds, to my quick curses!
Though not by war, by surfeit die your king,
As ours by murder, to make him a king!
Edward thy son, that now is Prince of Wales,
For Edward our son, that was Prince of Wales,
Die in his youth by like untimely violence!
Thyself a queen, for me that was a queen,

205. *Deck'd:* dressed.
stall'd: enthroned.
206. 'May your happiness come to an end long before you die.'

213. *cut off:* die before old age.

214. *charm:* spell, curse.
hag: witch.

218. *them:* heavenly powers.

223. *deep:* very cunning.

227. *elvish-mark'd:* marked at birth by evil spirits.
abortive: monstrous.
rooting: digging up with its snout.
hog: Richard's badge was a white boar.
228. *seal'd:* stamped with a seal, and thus 'fixed'.
nativity: birth.
229. *slave of nature:* mean and contemptible by nature.
230. *slander:* disgrace.
232. *rag:* something worthless: a vaguely contemptuous term.

233. *Margaret!* Richard completes the curse, intending to turn against her.
Ha? 'What did you say?' Richard pretends that she is calling to attra[ct] his attention.

Outlive thy glory, like my wretched self!
Long mayest thou live to wail thy children's death,
And see another, as I see thee now,
Deck'd in thy rights, as thou art stall'd in mine!
Long die thy happy days before thy death;
And, after many lengthen'd hours of grief,
Die neither mother, wife, nor England's Queen!
Rivers and Dorset, you were standers by,
And so wast thou, Lord Hastings, when my son
Was stabb'd with bloody daggers. God, I pray him,
That none of you may live his natural age,
But by some unlook'd accident cut off!

Gloucester

Have done thy charm, thou hateful wither'd hag.

Queen Margaret

And leave out thee? Stay, dog, for thou shalt hear me.
If heaven have any grievous plague in store
Exceeding those that I can wish upon thee,
O, let them keep it till thy sins be ripe,
And then hurl down their indignation
On thee, the troubler of the poor world's peace!
The worm of conscience still be-gnaw thy soul!
Thy friends suspect for traitors while thou liv'st,
And take deep traitors for thy dearest friends!
No sleep close up that deadly eye of thine,
Unless it be while some tormenting dream
Affrights thee with a hell of ugly devils!
Thou elvish-mark'd, abortive, rooting hog,
Thou that wast seal'd in thy nativity
The slave of nature and the son of hell,
Thou slander of thy heavy mother's womb,
Thou loathed issue of thy father's loins,
Thou rag of honour, thou detested—

Gloucester

Margaret!

Queen Margaret Richard!

Gloucester Ha?

234. *I cry thee mercy:* I beg your pardon.

237. *make the period:* bring to an end.

240. *painted:* imitation.
vain flourish: showy imitation.
241. *Why . . . sugar:* 'Why do you feed and encourage . . .?'
bottl'd: swollen (shaped like a bottle).

244-5. The day comes in Act IV, Scene iv.

246. *False-boding:* prophesying incorrectly.

247. 'Beware that you don't wear out our patience so that we do you some harm.'

249. 'If you got what you deserved you would be taught how to behave (before your queen).'

250. *do me duty:* kneel before me.

254. *malapert:* impudent.

255. Margaret compares him to a newly minted coin that people hardly yet realize is acceptable as money. He has only recently been created marquis (rank below duke and above earl or count).

Queen Margaret I call thee not.

Gloucester

I cry thee mercy then, for I did think
That thou hadst call'd me all these bitter names.

Queen Margaret

Why, so I did, but look'd for no reply.
O, let me make the period to my curse!

Gloucester

'Tis done by me, and ends in—Margaret.

Queen Elizabeth

Thus have you breath'd your curse against yourself.

Queen Margaret

Poor painted queen, vain flourish of my fortune!
Why strew'st thou sugar on that bottled spider
Whose deadly web ensnareth thee about?
Fool, fool! thou whet'st a knife to kill thyself.
The day will come that thou shalt wish for me
To help thee curse this poisonous bunch-back'd toad.

Hastings

False-boding woman, end thy frantic curse,
Lest to thy harm thou move our patience.

Queen Margaret

Foul shame upon you! you have all mov'd mine.

Rivers

Were you well serv'd, you would be taught your duty.

Queen Margaret

To serve me well you all should do me duty,
Teach me to be your queen and you my subjects.
O, serve me well, and teach yourselves that duty!

Dorset

Dispute not with her; she is lunatic.

Queen Margaret

Peace, Master Marquis, you are malapert;
Your fire-new stamp of honour is scarce current.
O, that your young nobility could judge
What 'twere to lose it and be miserable!

263. *Our aery:* Richard compares the family of York to eagles. An *aery* is an eagle's brood, as well as nest.
264. *scorns the sun:* Eagles were supposed to be able to look into the sun. Richard is saying that he and his brothers are not afraid of changes of fortune; they are used to the risk. The daring implied by this is certainly true of Richard himself.

275. *my hopes:* Her chief hope is that her son will succeed his father as king.
276. 'I have never had love shown to me—only hateful treatment, and my life of shame is the only sort of life I know.'

279. *princely:* The Duke of Buckingham was a descendant of Edward III, as were Henry VI, Edward IV, Richard III, and Henry VII.
280. *league:* association.
amity: friendship.
281. *Now . . . thee:* May good luck come to you.

283. *within the compass of:* included in.

They that stand high have many blasts to shake
them,
And if they fall they dash themselves to pieces.

Gloucester

Good counsel, marry; learn it, learn it, Marquis.

Dorset

It touches you, my lord, as much as me.

Gloucester

Ay, and much more; but I was born so high,
Our aery buildeth in the cedar's top,
And dallies with the wind, and scorns the sun.

Queen Margaret

And turns the sun to shade—alas! alas!
Witness my son, now in the shade of death,
Whose bright out-shining beams thy cloudy wrath
Hath in eternal darkness folded up.
Your aery buildeth in our aery's nest.
O God that seest it, do not suffer it;
As it is won with blood, lost be it so!

Buckingham

Peace, peace, for shame, if not for charity!

Queen Margaret

Urge neither charity nor shame to me.
Uncharitably with me have you dealt,
And shamefully my hopes by you are butcher'd.
My charity is outrage, life my shame;
And in that shame still live my sorrow's rage!

Buckingham

Have done, have done.

Queen Margaret

O princely Buckingham, I'll kiss thy hand
In sign of league and amity with thee.
Now fair befall thee and thy noble house!
Thy garments are not spotted with our blood,
Nor thou within the compass of my curse.

Buckingham

Nor no one here; for curses never pass

286. 'I refuse to think that they do not rise to heaven.'

287. *awake . . . peace:* rouse God from his calm peacefulness.

288-93. Though not a curse, this is another prophetic remark by Margaret that comes near fulfilment.

289. *Look when:* as soon as.

fawns: seems very affectionate. The comparison here is with a dog: a fawning dog is one that licks one's hand and is very obedient.

290. *rankle:* cause a wound that will go septic.

294. Richard butts in because he thinks that something is going on that he does not know about.

295. *respect:* take notice of.

296. *gentle counsel:* kind advice.

304. *muse:* wonder.

305-6. *by God's . . . wrong:* Do you think that Richard expects others to believe what he says so impudently?

306. *I repent:* We see why in a moment: he pretends to feel that all his efforts in fighting the Lancastrians have gone unrewarded.

309. 'But you gain all the benefits when others have wronged her.'

310-11. 'I was too eager in the past to help those (i.e. the king and his family), who now forget what I did for them.'

The lips of those that breathe them in the air.

Queen Margaret

I will not think but they ascend the sky
And there awake God's gentle-sleeping peace.
O Buckingham, take heed of yonder dog!
Look when he fawns, he bites; and when he bites,
His venom tooth will rankle to the death:
Have not to do with him, beware of him;
Sin, death, and hell, have set their marks on him,
And all their ministers attend on him.

Gloucester

What doth she say, my Lord of Buckingham?

Buckingham

Nothing that I respect, my gracious lord.

Queen Margaret

What, dost thou scorn me for my gentle counsel,
And soothe the devil that I warn thee from?
O, but remember this another day,
When he shall split thy very heart with sorrow,
And say poor Margaret was a prophetess!
Live each of you the subjects to his hate,
And he to yours, and all of you to God's!

Exit

Buckingham

My hair doth stand an end to hear her curses.

Rivers

And so doth mine. I muse why she's at liberty.

Gloucester

I cannot blame her; by God's holy Mother,
She hath had too much wrong; and I repent
My part thereof that I have done to her.

Queen Elizabeth

I never did her any to my knowledge.

Gloucester

Yet you have all the vantage of her wrong.
I was too hot to do somebody good

313. *frank'd up:* shut up in a pen. Clarence is compared to an animal being fattened ready for killing.

315-16. Rivers will say anything to please Richard.
scathe: injury.

317. *So . . . ever:* Richard refuses to quarrel any more and gives a gentle answer, though it is qualified in the next line.

322. *wait upon:* attend, accompany.
your Grace: i.e. Richard.

323-7. While reminding us of his method, and taking the Clarence story one stage further, Richard is congratulating himself and enjoying his success.
323. *brawl:* squabble. Richard does this of course to prevent others from starting to complain against him.
324. *set abroach:* set off.
325. 'I blame others who are held responsible for these serious crimes.'
327. 'I weep (for Clarence) in front of people who are silly enough to believe me.'
328. *Namely:* in particular.

331. *whet me:* encourage me. Richard is comparing himself with a sword being sharpened for use.

335. *naked villainy:* This suggests that Richard does not think that he is very subtle: if the others had any sense at all they would not be tricked.
336. *odd old ends:* any old scraps (of quotations from the Bible) that are not even consistent.

That is too cold in thinking of it now.
Marry, as for Clarence, he is well repaid;
He is frank'd up to fatting for his pains;
God pardon them that are the cause thereof!

Rivers

A virtuous and a Christian-like conclusion,
To pray for them that have done scathe to us!

Gloucester

So do I ever—[*Aside*] being well advis'd;
For had I curs'd now, I had curs'd myself.

Enter CATESBY

Catesby

Madam, his Majesty doth call for you,
And for your Grace, and you, my gracious lords.

Queen Elizabeth

Catesby, I come. Lords, will you go with me?

Rivers

We wait upon your Grace.

Exeunt all but GLOUCESTER

Gloucester

I do the wrong, and first begin to brawl.
The secret mischiefs that I set abroach
I lay unto the grievous charge of others.
Clarence, who I indeed have cast in darkness,
I do beweep to many simple gulls;
Namely, to Derby, Hastings, Buckingham;
And tell them 'tis the Queen and her allies
That stir the King against the Duke my brother.
Now they believe it, and withal whet me
To be reveng'd on Rivers, Dorset, Grey;
But then I sigh and, with a piece of Scripture,
Tell them that God bids us do good for evil.
And thus I clothe my naked villainy
With odd old ends stol'n forth of holy writ,
And seem a saint when most I play the devil.

338. *soft:* quietly now!

339. *hardy:* tough.
stout: brave.
340. *dispatch this thing:* There are two possible meanings: (1) do this job quickly; (2) kill this object, Clarence.
341. *the warrant:* a pass to his cell.

346. *obdurate:* stubborn, unmoved.
347. *well-spoken:* a persuasive speaker.
348. *mark:* pay attention to.
349. *prate:* chatter.
353-4. Although Richard would not agree with the murderers that talking is a waste of time, he adopts a very brisk, workmanlike manner with them, for the time for action has come.
353. *straight:* at once. We should say 'straight away.'

SCENE IV

This scene shows the cost of the kind of ruthless selfishness that we have just seen and that we shall see again. Clarence is meant to be typical of all those who break their oaths and look for their own advantage all the time, forgetting loyalty and honour and love, and in this scene he gets his reward: he suffers the terrifying dream and then is murdered. His dream portrays—with the skulls among the precious stones—the irony of worldly reward.

Not only is Clarence in his dream brought face to face with the truth about his past and his probable future, but when he pleads with the murderers he is made to accept the sinfulness of his self-seeking and faithlessness. The 'ordinary' men who come to kill him are not only Richard's agents but, in a sense, God's too. Their accusations against Clarence have more force for the audience than do the charges and counter-charges made by more 'important' people in the play, for *they* are moved by personal and political feelings against Clarence and each other, while the murderers are impersonal, as we expect justice to be.

Clarence's sufferings in this scene we should think of as not only his own, but what all the many guilty men and women in the play must suffer. Shakespeare will not need to go to such lengths to make his point again.

1. *heavily:* sadly.

Enter two MURDERERS

But, soft, here come my executioners.
How now, my hardy stout resolved mates!
Are you now going to dispatch this thing?

First Murderer

We are, my lord, and come to have the warrant,
That we may be admitted where he is.

Gloucester

Well thought upon; I have it here about me.

Gives the warrant

When you have done, repair to Crosby Place.
But, sirs, be sudden in the execution,
Withal obdurate, do not hear him plead;
For Clarence is well-spoken, and perhaps
May move your hearts to pity, if you mark him.

First Murderer

Tut, tut, my lord, we will not stand to prate;
Talkers are no good doers. Be assur'd
We go to use our hands and not our tongues.

Gloucester

Your eyes drop millstones when fools' eyes fall tears.
I like you, lads; about your business straight;
Go, go, dispatch.

First Murderer We will, my noble lord.

Exeunt

SCENE IV—*London. The Tower*

Enter CLARENCE *and* KEEPER

Keeper

Why looks your Grace so heavily to-day?

Clarence

O, I have pass'd a miserable night,

10. *Burgundy:* Here Clarence refers to land comprising what is today Holland and Belgium. Clarence's sister was married to the Duke of Burgundy who held this territory.

14. *cited up:* remembered and talked about.

17. *giddy:* unsteady.

19. *that thought . . . him:* who was trying to stop his fall.

27. *unvalued:* priceless.

32-3. The gems were like eyes in the sockets of the skull, flashing enticing and derisive looks at the skeletons around them.

So full of fearful dreams, of ugly sights,
That, as I am a Christian faithful man,
I would not spend another such a night
Though 'twere to buy a world of happy days—
So full of dismal terror was the time!

Keeper

What was your dream, my lord? I pray you tell me.

Clarence

Methoughts that I had broken from the Tower
And was embark'd to cross to Burgundy;
And in my company my brother Gloucester,
Who from my cabin tempted me to walk
Upon the hatches. Thence we look'd toward England,
And cited up a thousand heavy times,
During the wars of York and Lancaster,
That had befall'n us. As we pac'd along
Upon the giddy footing of the hatches,
Methought that Gloucester stumbled, and in falling
Struck me, that thought to stay him, overboard
Into the tumbling billows of the main.
O Lord, methought what pain it was to drown,
What dreadful noise of waters in my ears,
What sights of ugly death within my eyes!
Methoughts I saw a thousand fearful wrecks,
A thousand men that fishes gnaw'd upon,
Wedges of gold, great anchors, heaps of pearl,
Inestimable stones, unvalued jewels,
All scatter'd in the bottom of the sea;
Some lay in dead men's skulls, and in the holes
Where eyes did once inhabit there were crept,
As 'twere in scorn of eyes, reflecting gems,
That woo'd the slimy bottom of the deep
And mock'd the dead bones that lay scatter'd by.

Keeper

Had you such leisure in the time of death
To gaze upon these secrets of the deep?

37. *yield the ghost:* let my soul leave my body.

45. *flood:* the river Styx across which, according to Greek mythology, the dead passed into the lower world.
46. *sour:* gloomy, sullen.
ferryman: Charon, who rowed the dead across the river Styx to Hades, according to ancient Greek legend.
48. *stranger soul:* Clarence was a stranger because he had only just come to hell.
50. *scourge:* punishment.
perjury: Clarence had broken his promise that he would support Warwick.

53. *shadow:* the ghost of Edward, son of Henry VI.

55. *fleeting:* changeable, fickle.

57. *Furies:* in Greek mythology, spirits that punish men on the gods' behalf.

59. *Environ'd:* surrounded.

61. *season:* a period of time.

Clarence

Methought I had; and often did I strive
To yield the ghost, but still the envious flood
Stopp'd in my soul and would not let it forth
To find the empty, vast, and wand'ring air;
But smother'd it within my panting bulk,
Who almost burst to belch it in the sea.

Keeper

Awak'd you not in this sore agony?

Clarence

No, no, my dream was lengthen'd after life.
O, then began the tempest to my soul!
I pass'd, methought, the melancholy flood
With that sour ferryman which poets write of,
Unto the kingdom of perpetual night.
The first that there did greet my stranger soul
Was my great father-in-law, renowned Warwick,
Who spake aloud 'What scourge for perjury
Can this dark monarchy afford false Clarence?'
And so he vanish'd. Then came wand'ring by
A shadow like an angel, with bright hair
Dabbled in blood, and he shriek'd out aloud
'Clarence is come—false, fleeting, perjur'd Clarence,
That stabb'd me in the field by Tewksbury.
Seize on him, Furies, take him unto torment!'
With that, methoughts, a legion of foul fiends
Environ'd me, and howled in mine ears
Such hideous cries that, with the very noise,
I trembling wak'd, and for a season after
Could not believe but that I was in hell,
Such terrible impression made my dream.

Keeper

No marvel, lord, though it affrighted you;
I am afraid, methinks, to hear you tell it.

Clarence

Ah, Keeper, Keeper, I have done these things
That now give evidence against my soul

68. *requites:* repays.

73. *I prithee:* I beg you.

74. *fain would:* would like to.

76-83. As Brakenbury looks at the sleeping Clarence, he thinks about his change of fortune. He expresses himself in a very matter-of-fact way, in marked contrast with the recent highly dramatic outpourings of Clarence.

76. *breaks seasons:* puts things out of their usual order.

80. *unfelt imaginations:* the pleasures that other people imagine that princes enjoy, but which in fact princes never feel.

82-3. 'There is no difference between members of royal families and the humble poor except that the former are well-known.'

Stage Direction. In Elizabethan plays, servants were often brisk, witty men like these two, and being 'low' characters they are made to speak in prose, not verse.

91. *commission:* orders.

For Edward's sake, and see how he requites me!
O God! If my deep prayers cannot appease Thee,
But Thou wilt be aveng'd on my misdeeds,
Yet execute Thy wrath in me alone;
O, spare my guiltless wife and my poor children!
Keeper, I prithee sit by me awhile;
My soul is heavy, and I fain would sleep.

Keeper

I will, my lord. God give your Grace good rest.

CLARENCE *sleeps*

Enter BRAKENBURY *the Lieutenant*

Brakenbury

Sorrow breaks seasons and reposing hours,
Makes the night morning and the noontide night.
Princes have but their titles for their glories,
An outward honour for an inward toil;
And for unfelt imaginations
They often feel a world of restless cares,
So that between their titles and low name
There's nothing differs but the outward fame.

Enter the two MURDERERS

First Murderer

Ho! who's here?

Brakenbury

What wouldst thou, fellow, and how cam'st thou hither?

First Murderer

I would speak with Clarence, and I came hither on my legs.

Brakenbury

What, so brief?

Second Murderer

'Tis better, sir, than to be tedious. Let him see our commission and talk no more.

BRAKENBURY *reads it*

93-4. Brakenbury does not want to know what is going on. Does this show common-sense, or is he guilty because he does not intervene?

96. *and there:* perhaps on a table. Brakenbury is being careful not to have any contact with the men.

102. *great judgment-day:* This is the day, according to Christian teaching, when God will call all souls, living and dead, to give an account of their lives. The wicked will be punished and the good rewarded.

106. *remorse:* doubt, scruple.

108. *warrant:* The pass they carried would also be their instructions to kill Clarence.
damn'd: condemned to suffer in hell, after death, as punishment for his sins.
111. *resolute:* determined, firm.

Brakenbury

I am, in this, commanded to deliver
The noble Duke of Clarence to your hands.
I will not reason what is meant hereby,
Because I will be guiltless from the meaning.
There lies the Duke asleep; and there the keys.
I'll to the King and signify to him
That thus I have resign'd to you my charge.

First Murderer

You may, sir; 'tis a point of wisdom. Fare you well.

Exeunt BRAKENBURY *and* KEEPER

Second Murderer

What, shall I stab him as he sleeps?

First Murderer

No; he'll say 'twas done cowardly, when he wakes.

Second Murderer

Why, he shall never wake until the great judgment-day.

First Murderer

Why, then he'll say we stabb'd him sleeping.

Second Murderer

The urging of that word judgment hath bred a kind of remorse in me.

First Murderer

What, art thou afraid?

Second Murderer

Not to kill him, having a warrant; but to be damn'd for killing him, from the which no warrant can defend me.

First Murderer

I thought thou hadst been resolute.

Second Murderer

So I am, to let him live.

First Murderer

I'll back to the Duke of Gloucester and tell him so.

114-15. *passionate humour:* feelings of pity or sympathy.

115-16. *it was . . . twenty:* it usually only keeps hold of me for as long as it takes to count up to twenty.

118. *dregs:* the last drops of drink left in a cup.

125. *conscience flies out:* He means that his partner's conscience will be troublesome again.

126-7. *there's few . . . it:* There are very few people who care at all about conscience.

129. *meddle with it:* have anything to do with it.

133. *shamefac'd:* bashful, shy.

135. *by chance I found:* The murderer was about to confess that he stole the purse; but shame makes him confess only to the less serious crime.

136-7. *It is . . . thing:* Beggars, and other undesirable people, were turned out of towns and left to go to be a trouble in other places.

138. *live well:* enjoy life.

Second Murderer

Nay, I prithee, stay a little. I hope this passionate humour of mine will change; it was wont to hold me but while one tells twenty.

First Murderer

How dost thou feel thyself now?

Second Murderer

Faith, some certain dregs of conscience are yet within me.

First Murderer

Remember our reward, when the deed's done.

Second Murderer

Zounds, he dies; I had forgot the reward.

First Murderer

Where's thy conscience now?

Second Murderer

O, in the Duke of Gloucester's purse!

First Murderer

When he opens his purse to give us our reward, thy conscience flies out.

Second Murderer

'Tis no matter; let it go; there's few or none will entertain it.

First Murderer

What if it come to thee again?

Second Murderer

I'll not meddle with it—it makes a man a coward: a man cannot steal, but it accuseth him; a man cannot swear, but it checks him; a man cannot lie with his neighbour's wife, but it detects him. 'Tis a blushing shamefac'd spirit that mutinies in a man's bosom; it fills a man full of obstacles: it made me once restore a purse of gold that—by chance I found. It beggars any man that keeps it. It is turn'd out of towns and cities for a dangerous thing; and every man that means to live well endeavours to trust to himself and live without it.

142. *Take the devil in thy mind:* arrest your devil of a conscience.

143. *would insinuate . . . sigh:* 'he would creep into your favour, and you would only sigh as a result.' The sigh might be because he felt sorry for his sins, or because he wanted to be doing what others were doing.

144. *strong-fram'd:* well-built.
prevail with me: beat me in a fight.

145. *tall:* brave.

147. *Take . . . costard:* hit him on the head.

148. *chop:* pitch, throw.
malmsey-butt: a barrel of malmsey, a strong, sweet wine.

150. *device:* ingenious idea.
sop: piece of cake or bread floating in a drink.

155. *anon:* very soon.

157. Because they are where they are, there is nothing to choose between the murderer and the duke, as Brakenbury had reflected in his speech. They are, too, equal in the sight of God. In some ways, as the murderer goes on to show, he is a better man, and more moral than Clarence.

First Murderer

Zounds, 'tis even now at my elbow, persuading me not to kill the Duke.

Second Murderer

Take the devil in thy mind and believe him not; he would insinuate with thee but to make thee sigh.

First Murderer

I am strong-fram'd; he cannot prevail with me.

Second Murderer

Spoke like a tall man that respects thy reputation. Come, shall we fall to work?

First Murderer

Take him on the costard with the hilts of thy sword, and then chop him in the malmsey-butt in the next room.

Second Murderer

O excellent device! and make a sop of him.

First Murderer

Soft! he wakes.

Second Murderer

Strike!

First Murderer

No, we'll reason with him.

Clarence

Where art thou, Keeper? Give me a cup of wine.

Second Murderer

You shall have wine enough, my lord, anon.

Clarence

In God's name, what art thou?

First Murderer

A man, as you are.

Clarence

But not as I am, royal.

Second Murderer

Nor you as we are, loyal.

Clarence

Thy voice is thunder, but thy looks are humble.

161. To pass the responsibility to others is one way of trying to avoid guilt. The murderers, when face to face with their victim, both lose some of their determination.
162. *darkly:* with a frown, gloomily.

171. *the King:* No doubt Richard has convinced the murderers that his orders are in accordance with King Edward's wishes.

172. In the past Clarence has been forgiven for certain acts of disloyalty. Do you think he is smug when he says this, or only desperate, or unaware of who is really in power now?

174. *drawn forth . . . men:* chosen from a whole world full of men

176. Although Clarence is aware of his guilt, he is still wanting proof that the world will accept.
177. *lawful quest:* properly constituted court.

180. *convict:* convicted.

182. *to have redemption:* to be saved from damnation on the grea judgment-day.

185. *is damnable:* will condemn you to hell.

First Murderer
My voice is now the King's, my looks mine own.
Clarence
How darkly and how deadly dost thou speak!
Your eyes do menace me. Why look you pale?
Who sent you hither? Wherefore do you come?
Second Murderer
To, to, to—
Clarence
To murder me?
Both Murderers
Ay, ay.
Clarence
You scarcely have the hearts to tell me so,
And therefore cannot have the hearts to do it.
Wherein, my friends, have I offended you?
First Murderer
Offended us you have not, but the King.
Clarence
I shall be reconcil'd to him again.
Second Murderer
Never, my lord; therefore prepare to die.
Clarence
Are you drawn forth among a world of men
To slay the innocent? What is my offence?
Where is the evidence that doth accuse me?
What lawful quest have given their verdict up
Unto the frowning judge, or who pronounc'd
The bitter sentence of poor Clarence' death?
Before I be convict by course of law,
To threaten me with death is most unlawful.
I charge you, as you hope to have redemption
By Christ's dear blood shed for our grievous sins,
That you depart and lay no hands on me.
The deed you undertake is damnable.
First Murderer
What we will do, we do upon command.

188. *Erroneous vassals:* sinful servants.
King of kings: God.
189. *tables of his law:* the Ten Commandments, God's moral code revealed to Moses in the Old Testament.
191. *Spurn at:* kick aside with contempt.
edict: law.

196. Clarence swore an oath in church that he would fight on Henry VI's side.

200. *thy sov'reign's son:* Prince Edward, Henry VI's son.

203. *in such dear degree:* so extremely.

213. 'Who told you to kill on God's behalf?'

215. *novice:* Tewkesbury was Prince Edward's first battle.

Second Murderer

And he that hath commanded is our king.

Clarence

Erroneous vassals! the great King of kings
Hath in the tables of his law commanded
That thou shalt do no murder. Will you then
Spurn at his edict and fulfil a man's?
Take heed; for he holds vengeance in his hand
To hurl upon their heads that break his law.

Second Murderer

And that same vengeance doth he hurl on thee
For false forswearing, and for murder too;
Thou didst receive the sacrament to fight
In quarrel of the house of Lancaster.

First Murderer

And like a traitor to the name of God
Didst break that vow; and with thy treacherous blade
Unripp'dst the bowels of thy sov'reign's son.

Second Murderer

Whom thou wast sworn to cherish and defend.

First Murderer

How canst thou urge God's dreadful law to us,
When thou hast broke it in such dear degree?

Clarence

Alas! for whose sake did I that ill deed?
For Edward, for my brother, for his sake.
He sends you not to murder me for this,
For in that sin he is as deep as I.
If God will be avenged for the deed,
O, know you yet He doth it publicly.
Take not the quarrel from His pow'rful arm;
He needs no indirect or lawless course
To cut off those that have offended Him.

First Murderer

Who made thee then a bloody minister
When gallant-springing brave Plantagenet,
That princely novice, was struck dead by thee?

220. This ironical line shows how skilful Richard's deception could be.
221. *meed:* reward.

224. *tidings:* news.

227. *Ay, so we will:* a grimly ironical remark. The murderers will go to Richard to report Clarence's death.

233. *lesson'd:* instructed.

234. *kind:* Clarence means 'gentle and sympathetic', but the murderer answers as though he had meant s other meaning of 'natural'.

239. *delivery:* release from prison.

Clarence
My brother's love, the devil, and my rage.
First Murderer
Thy brother's love, our duty, and thy faults,
Provoke us hither now to slaughter thee.
Clarence
If you do love my brother, hate not me;
I am his brother, and I love him well.
If you are hir'd for meed, go back again,
And I will send you to my brother Gloucester,
Who shall reward you better for my life
Than Edward will for tidings of my death.
Second Murderer
You are deceiv'd: your brother Gloucester hates
you.
Clarence
O, no, he loves me, and he holds me dear.
Go you to him from me.
First Murderer Ay, so we will.
Clarence
Tell him when that our princely father York
Bless'd his three sons with his victorious arm
And charg'd us from his soul to love each other,
He little thought of this divided friendship.
Bid Gloucester think of this, and he will weep.
First Murderer
Ay, millstones; as he lesson'd us to weep.
Clarence
O, do not slander him, for he is kind.
First Murderer
Right, as snow in harvest. Come, you deceive
yourself:
'Tis he that sends us to destroy you here.
Clarence
It cannot be; for he bewept my fortune
And hugg'd me in his arms, and swore with sobs
That he would labour my delivery.

241. *thraldom:* slavery.

242. The Second Murderer is still the more humane, as he continues to be until the end. This line contrasts well with the harshness of the First Murderer.

245. 'Are you so ignorant of the harm you are doing your own souls (which will be damned)?'

247. *set you on:* gave you orders.

249. The murderer seems about to give way to the pleading.

253. *pent:* shut up.

255. *entreat:* beg.

256. *My friend:* Clarence is speaking to the Second Murderer.

261. The murderer is probably warning him of the attack. If he was intending to distract Clarence's attention to make the murder easier he would surely have done the stabbing himself.

264. *desperately:* rashly, not taking any notice of possible consequences.

First Murderer
Why, so he doth, when he delivers you
From this earth's thraldom to the joys of heaven.

Second Murderer
Make peace with God, for you must die, my lord.

Clarence
Have you that holy feeling in your souls
To counsel me to make my peace with God,
And are you yet to your own souls so blind
That you will war with God by murd'ring me?
O, sirs, consider: they that set you on
To do this deed will hate you for the deed.

Second Murderer
What shall we do?

Clarence Relent, and save your souls.

First Murderer
Relent! No, 'tis cowardly and womanish.

Clarence
Not to relent is beastly, savage, devilish.
Which of you, if you were a prince's son,
Being pent from liberty as I am now,
If two such murderers as yourselves came to you,
Would not entreat for life?
My friend, I spy some pity in thy looks;
O, if thine eye be not a flatterer,
Come thou on my side and entreat for me—
As you would beg were you in my distress.
A begging prince what beggar pities not?

Second Murderer
Look behind you, my lord.

First Murderer [*Stabbing him*]
Take that, and that. If all this will not do, I'll drown you in the malmsey-butt within.

Exit with the body

Second Murderer
A bloody deed, and desperately dispatch'd!

265. *Pilate:* When Jesus was accused before Pilate, the Roman governor, Pilate washed his hands as a sign that he did not want to be involved.

276. *this:* the murder.

How fain, like Pilate, would I wash my hands
Of this most grievous murder!

Re-enter FIRST MURDERER

First Murderer
How now, what mean'st thou that thou help'st me not?
By heavens, the Duke shall know how slack you have been!

Second Murderer
I would he knew that I had sav'd his brother!
Take thou the fee, and tell him what I say;
For I repent me that the Duke is slain.

Exit

First Murderer
So do not I. Go, coward as thou art.
Well, I'll go hide the body in some hole,
Till that the Duke give order for his burial;
And when I have my meed, I will away;
For this will out, and then I must not stay.

Exit

ACT TWO

SCENE I

The scene opens towards the end of the meeting round King Edward's sick-bed that follows on Act I, Scene iii, and shows Richard's first *public* triumph. He has already won over the Lady Anne, but now he completes his first major scheme, and fills his opponents with fear.

2. *peers:* lords.
united league: association and agreement.
3. *embassage:* message.
4. *hence:* i.e. from this world.

8. 'Don't go on disguising your hatred; admit it and then make friends.'

9. *purg'd:* cleared of.
grudging: envious.

11. 'May my good fortune in life depend upon my speaking the truth now.'

12. *dally:* play; do things without being serious about them.

14. *Confound . . . falsehood:* punish you for your secret lies.
award: order.

ACT TWO

SCENE I—*London. The palace*

Flourish. Enter KING EDWARD *sick,* QUEEN ELIZABETH, DORSET, RIVERS, HASTINGS, BUCKINGHAM, GREY *and* OTHERS

King Edward
Why, so. Now have I done a good day's work.
You peers, continue this united league.
I every day expect an embassage
From my Redeemer to redeem me hence;
And more at peace my soul shall part to heaven,
Since I have made my friends at peace on earth.
Hastings and Rivers, take each other's hand;
Dissemble not your hatred, swear your love.

Rivers
By heaven, my soul is purg'd from grudging hate;
And with my hand I seal my true heart's love.

Hastings
So thrive I, as I truly swear the like!

King Edward
Take heed you dally not before your king;
Lest He that is the supreme King of kings
Confound your hidden falsehood and award
Either of you to be the other's end.

Hastings
So prosper I, as I swear perfect love!

Rivers
And I, as I love Hastings with my heart!

King Edward
Madam, yourself is not exempt from this;
Nor you, son Dorset; Buckingham, nor you:

20. 'You have been enemies of each other.'

22. *unfeignedly:* sincerely.

32-40. Buckingham, we now can guess, is sealing his own fate here.
32-4. *Whenever Buckingham . . . yours:* When Buckingham shows hatred towards you, or anything but dutiful affection for you and your family.
33. *but:* and not.

37. *and most assured:* This could mean, 'and need to be most certain', or, 'and am most certain'.
38. *Deep:* very cunning.
hollow: insincere.
guile: insincerity.

41. *cordial:* medicine or beverage.

43. *wanteth:* is missing.
44. *period:* conclusion.

You have been factious one against the other.
Wife, love Lord Hastings, let him kiss your hand;
And what you do, do it unfeignedly.

Queen Elizabeth

There, Hastings; I will never more remember
Our former hatred, so thrive I and mine!

King Edward

Dorset, embrace him; Hastings, love Lord Marquis.

Dorset

This interchange of love, I here protest,
Upon my part shall be inviolable.

Hastings

And so swear I.

They embrace

King Edward

Now, princely Buckingham, seal thou this league
With thy embracements to my wife's allies,
And make me happy in your unity.

Buckingham [*To the* QUEEN]

Whenever Buckingham doth turn his hate
Upon your Grace, but with all duteous love
Doth cherish you and yours, God punish me
With hate in those where I expect most love!
When I have most need to employ a friend
And most assured that he is a friend,
Deep, hollow, treacherous, and full of guile,
Be he unto me! This do I beg of God
When I am cold in love to you or yours.

They embrace

King Edward

A pleasing cordial, princely Buckingham,
Is this thy vow unto my sickly heart.
There wanteth now our brother Gloucester here
To make the blessed period of this peace.

45. *in good time:* at the right moment.

47-8. Richard is apparently feeling very friendly to all.

52. *swelling:* filled with anger.
wrong-incensed: made angry by the wrongs done to them.

53-74. This speech is another of those coming from Richard in his character of humble Christian. He plays exactly the part that those who are most important to him at this point in the story want him to play.
54. *heap:* great company.
55. *false intelligence:* incorrect information.
surmise: guess.
57. *unwittingly:* without knowing.

66. 'If ever there was any ill-feeling between us.'

68. *all:* completely.
without desert: i.e. Richard does not deserve their hatred.

72. *jot:* a very small amount.
at odds: in disagreement.
74. Richard's line of superb conceit and hypocrisy apparently deceives even his keenest enemy, Elizabeth.
humility: humanity, love for all other men and women.

Buckingham
And, in good time,
Here comes Sir Richard Ratcliff and the Duke.

Enter GLOUCESTER *and* RATCLIFF

Gloucester
Good morrow to my sovereign king and queen;
And, princely peers, a happy time of day!
King Edward
Happy, indeed, as we have spent the day.
Gloucester, we have done deeds of charity,
Made peace of enmity, fair love of hate,
Between these swelling wrong-incensed peers.
Gloucester
A blessed labour, my most sovereign lord.
Among this princely heap, if any here,
By false intelligence or wrong surmise,
Hold me a foe—
If I unwittingly, or in my rage,
Have aught committed that is hardly borne
To any in this presence, I desire
To reconcile me to his friendly peace:
'Tis death to me to be at enmity;
I hate it, and desire all good men's love.
First, madam, I entreat true peace of you,
Which I will purchase with my duteous service;
Of you, my noble cousin Buckingham,
If ever any grudge were lodg'd between us;
Of you, and you, Lord Rivers, and of Dorset,
That all without desert have frown'd on me;
Of you, Lord Woodville, and, Lord Scales, of you;
Dukes, earls, lords, gentlemen—indeed, of all.
I do not know that Englishman alive
With whom my soul is any jot at odds
More than the infant that is born to-night.
I thank my God for my humility.

76. *compounded:* brought to an end.

79-82. Richard has put his enemies in the wrong and himself in the virtuous position. Whether his enemies believe him for long does not matter; he has outwitted them and it is now harder for them to convince others that Richard has done wrong.
80. *flouted:* taunted, treated with contempt.

88. *the order:* i.e. the order that he should be executed.

90. *a winged Mercury:* an extremely swift messenger. Mercury was the messenger of the gods in Roman mythology, and had wings on his heels.
91. *tardy:* slow.
countermand: second order contradicting the first.
92. 'that was so slow that he was buried before it arrived.' (*lag* = late).
93. *less noble and less loyal:* Richard has soon turned back to his attacks on the queen's family, whom he is accusing here of being responsible for Clarence's death.
94. *an not in blood:* even if they are not close relations.
96. *current:* moving about freely.

Queen Elizabeth
A holy day shall this be kept hereafter.
I would to God all strifes were well compounded.
My sovereign lord, I do beseech your Highness
To take our brother Clarence to your grace.
Gloucester
Why, madam, have I offer'd love for this,
To be so flouted in this royal presence?
Who knows not that the gentle Duke is dead?

They all start

You do him injury to scorn his corse.
King Edward
Who knows not he is dead! Who knows he is?
Queen Elizabeth
All-seeing heaven, what a world is this!
Buckingham
Look I so pale, Lord Dorset, as the rest?
Dorset
Ay, my good lord; and no man in the presence
But his red colour hath forsook his cheeks.
King Edward
Is Clarence dead? The order was revers'd.
Gloucester
But he, poor man, by your first order died,
And that a winged Mercury did bear;
Some tardy cripple bare the countermand
That came too lag to see him buried.
God grant that some, less noble and less loyal,
Nearer in bloody thoughts, an not in blood,
Deserve not worse than wretched Clarence did,
And yet go current from suspicion!

Enter DERBY

Derby
A boon, my sovereign, for my service done!

101. 'The life of my servant, which he has been condemned to lose.'

106. *My . . . man:* Edward means, of course that Clarence killed no one in a private quarrel, though he must have killed men in battle. *his . . . thought:* i.e. he never did the treacherous acts he planned to do.
108. *sued:* pleaded.
109. *bid . . . advis'd:* advised me to act differently, not to execute Clarence.

112. *The mighty Warwick:* Richard Neville, Earl of Warwick, known as 'Warwick the King-maker'; also father of Anne.

114. *Oxford:* a nobleman fighting with the Lancastrian forces.

117. *lap:* wrap.

119. *thin and naked:* wearing few clothes.

122. *grace:* goodness.

124-5. *defac'd . . . Redeemer:* done harm to a man, who was made in the image of God.

129. *ungracious:* without God's grace.

King Edward
I prithee, peace; my soul is full of sorrow.
Derby
I will not rise unless your Highness hear me.
King Edward
Then say at once what is it thou requests.
Derby
The forfeit, sovereign, of my servant's life;
Who slew to-day a riotous gentleman
Lately attendant on the Duke of Norfolk.
King Edward
Have I a tongue to doom my brother's death,
And shall that tongue give pardon to a slave?
My brother kill'd no man—his fault was thought,
And yet his punishment was bitter death.
Who sued to me for him? Who, in my wrath,
Kneel'd at my feet, and bid me be advis'd?
Who spoke of brotherhood? Who spoke of love?
Who told me how the poor soul did forsake
The mighty Warwick and did fight for me?
Who told me, in the field at Tewksbury
When Oxford had me down, he rescued me
And said 'Dear Brother, live, and be a king'?
Who told me, when we both lay in the field
Frozen almost to death, how he did lap me
Even in his garments, and did give himself,
All thin and naked, to the numb cold night?
All this from my remembrance brutish wrath
Sinfully pluck'd, and not a man of you
Had so much gracc to put it in my mind.
But when your carters or your waiting-vassals
Have done a drunken slaughter and defac'd
The precious image of our dear Redeemer,
You straight are on your knees for pardon, pardon;
And I, unjustly too, must grant it you. [DERBY *rises*]
But for my brother not a man would speak;
Nor I, ungracious, speak unto myself

131. *beholding:* obliged for some help.

133-4. This is another suggestion that the misfortunes that come to the people in the story are willed by God as a punishment for their sins.
134. *mine, and yours:* my family and your families.
135. To help the king in this way was one of the Lord Chamberlain's duties.
closet: a small room.

136. *This:* Edward's grief and all his troubles.
136-7. We already know that *all* turned pale at the news (lines 85-7), presumably from fear of what Richard might be able to make of the situation, and realizing that they had been tricked, rather than from guilty consciences. We can see this speech as a warning to other nobles to think about whose side they are on.
139. *urge:* strongly advocate;
still: at all times.

142. 'We will accompany your Grace.'

SCENE II

This is the first of the two scenes in the play in which the women, in addition to taking part in new events and telling the audience what is happening, comment on and concentrate the audience's attention on the actions that have taken place. This was the job of the Chorus in classical Greek plays. Here it is done in very artificial verse, with much repetition. The result is like music in its effect: the creation of emotion by a pattern of sounds. This kind of poetry is clearly very different from the poetry of Clarence's dream (Act I, Scene iv, lines 2-63).

Stage Direction. The Duchess of York is the mother of King Edward IV, Clarence, and Richard.

3-7. Children are often shown like this in Shakespeare: more direct and clear-sighted than their elders.

For him, poor soul. The proudest of you all
Have been beholding to him in his life;
Yet none of you would once beg for his life.
O God, I fear thy justice will take hold
On me, and you, and mine, and yours, for this!
Come, Hastings, help me to my closet. Ah, poor
Clarence!

Exeunt some with KING *and* QUEEN

Gloucester

This is the fruits of rashness. Mark'd you not
How that the guilty kindred of the Queen
Look'd pale when they did hear of Clarence' death?
O, they did urge it still unto the King!
God will revenge it. Come, lords, will you go
To comfort Edward with our company?

Buckingham

We wait upon your Grace.

Exeunt

SCENE II—*London. The palace*

Enter the old DUCHESS OF YORK, *with the* SON *and* DAUGHTER *of* CLARENCE

Son

Good grandam, tell us, is our father dead?

Duchess of York

No, boy.

Daughter

Why do you weep so oft, and beat your breast,
And cry 'O Clarence, my unhappy son!'?

Son

Why do you look on us, and shake your head,

8. *cousins:* a term used for all close relations, by princes and nobles.

10. *as loath:* for I should be sorry.
11. *lost:* wasted.

14. *importune:* pester.

18. *incapable:* not able to understand.
shallow: naive, simple.

20-6. Richard is prepared to deceive everyone, and indirectly to corrupt anyone.

22. *Devis'd impeachments:* invented charges of treason.

24. *kindly:* with the affection natural to an uncle.

27. *steal . . . shape:* borrow such a disguise, to make you look a gentl person.
28. *vizor:* a mask. Here *virtuous vizor* means appearance of virtue.
vice: evil. But Vice was also a character in the Morality plays; so *shape*, *vizor*, and *vice* are all terms from play-acting, and therefor appropriate metaphors in describing Richard.
30. *dugs:* breasts.

And call us orphans, wretches, castaways,
If that our noble father were alive?

Duchess of York

My pretty cousins, you mistake me both;
I do lament the sickness of the King,
As loath to lose him, not your father's death;
It were lost sorrow to wail one that's lost.

Son

Then you conclude, my grandam, he is dead.
The King mine uncle is to blame for it.
God will revenge it; whom I will importune
With earnest prayers all to that effect.

Daughter

And so will I.

Duchess of York

Peace, children, peace! The King doth love you well.
Incapable and shallow innocents,
You cannot guess who caus'd your father's death.

Son

Grandam, we can; for my good uncle Gloucester
Told me the King, provok'd to it by the Queen,
Devis'd impeachments to imprison him.
And when my uncle told me so, he wept,
And pitied me, and kindly kiss'd my cheek;
Bade me rely on him as on my father,
And he would love me dearly as a child.

Duchess of York

Ah, that deceit should steal such gentle shape,
And with a virtuous vizor hide deep vice!
He is my son; ay, and therein my shame;
Yet from my dugs he drew not this deceit.

Son

Think you my uncle did dissemble, grandam?

Duchess of York

Ay, boy.

Son

I cannot think it. Hark! what noise is this?

Stage Direction. *with her hair . . . ears:* Such disorderly appearance was a conventional way of showing grief.

34-5. 'Who dares to stop me from weeping and wailing and complaining about my misfortunes?'

38. *rude:* violent and noisy.
38-9. *scene . . . act:* These words continue the theatrical metaphor.

39. 'To complete the series of violent acts' or perhaps 'To do something violent to draw attention to my distress.'

41-2. 'Why should others continue to live when he has died?' Metaphors of growing trees and plants are very common in Shakespeare's history plays.
43. *If you . . . lament:* If you mean to stay alive, you must weep (either because you are bound to as a matter of duty, or because you will be unable to avoid doing so in such a dreadful world).
46. *kingdom . . . night:* This is not a Christian idea. The queen seems to be confusing the gloom of her world without her husband with the darkness of the next world.
47-8. 'As your husband was closely related to me, I share your grief.' *Title* and *interest* are legal terms suggesting ownership.

50. *his images:* reflections of him, i.e. his sons.

51. *two . . . semblance:* two princes who were like him.

53. *false glass:* a distorted reflection, i.e. Richard.

60. *moiety . . . moan:* half the reason I have to grieve.

61. *overgo:* exceed, overwhelm.

62. *aunt:* Queen Elizabeth.

Enter QUEEN ELIZABETH, *with her hair about her ears;* RIVERS *and* DORSET *after her*

Queen Elizabeth

Ah, who shall hinder me to wail and weep,
To chide my fortune, and torment myself?
I'll join with black despair against my soul
And to myself become an enemy.

Duchess of York

What means this scene of rude impatience?

Queen Elizabeth

To make an act of tragic violence.
Edward, my lord, thy son, our king, is dead.
Why grow the branches when the root is gone?
Why wither not the leaves that want their sap?
If you will live, lament; if die, be brief,
That our swift-winged souls may catch the King's,
Or like obedient subjects follow him
To his new kingdom of ne'er-changing night.

Duchess of York

Ah, so much interest have I in thy sorrow
As I had title in thy noble husband!
I have bewept a worthy husband's death,
And liv'd with looking on his images;
But now two mirrors of his princely semblance
Are crack'd in pieces by malignant death,
And I for comfort have but one false glass,
That grieves me when I see my shame in him.
Thou art a widow, yet thou art a mother
And hast the comfort of thy children left;
But death hath snatch'd my husband from mine arms
And pluck'd two crutches from my feeble hands—
Clarence and Edward. O, what cause have I—
Thine being but a moiety of my moan—
To overgo thy woes and drown thy cries?

Son

Ah, aunt, you wept not for our father's death!

63. *kindred:* as members of his family.

65. *widow-dolour:* sorrow in being a widow.

67. *barren . . . complaints:* sterile, empty of expressions of grief.

68. 'Let all rivers pour their waters through my eyes.'

69. *watery moon:* the moon that controls the tides of the sea.

74. *stay:* support.

81. *parcell'd:* separate and confined to each one of them.

88. *pamper:* indulge, spoil as a child is spoilt.

How can we aid you with our kindred tears?

Daughter

Our fatherless distress was left unmoan'd;
Your widow-dolour likewise be unwept!

Queen Elizabeth

Give me no help in lamentation;
I am not barren to bring forth complaints.
All springs reduce their currents to mine eyes
That I, being govern'd by the watery moon,
May send forth plenteous tears to drown the world!
Ah for my husband, for my dear Lord Edward!

Children

Ah for our father, for our dear Lord Clarence!

Duchess of York

Alas for both, both mine, Edward and Clarence!

Queen Elizabeth

What stay had I but Edward? and he's gone.

Children

What stay had we but Clarence? and he's gone.

Duchess of York

What stays had I but they? and they are gone.

Queen Elizabeth

Was never widow had so dear a loss.

Children

Were never orphans had so dear a loss.

Duchess of York

Was never mother had so dear a loss.
Alas, I am the mother of these griefs!
Their woes are parcell'd, mine is general.
She for an Edward weeps, and so do I:
I for a Clarence weep, so doth not she.
These babes for Clarence weep, and so do I:
I for an Edward weep, so do not they.
Alas, you three on me, threefold distress'd,
Pour all your tears! I am your sorrow's nurse,
And I will pamper it with lamentation.

94. 'It is much worse to oppose heaven's will in this way.'

95. *For:* just because.

97. *straight:* immediately.

100. *living Edward:* her son, Edward, Prince of Wales.

101. *Sister:* Richard is carrying out his promise made in Act I, Scene i, line 109: *Were it to call King Edward's widow sister.*

107. *meekness:* humility.

109-11. Richard's sarcastic, insolent aside is funny; but it suggests that perhaps he has not noticed the sternness, or even sarcasm, of his mother's words.

110. *butt end:* the last bit.

112. *cloudy:* sorrowful, sad.

113. 'That share this great burden of sorrow.'

115-16. More metaphors of growth, linking human affairs with the natural world.

Dorset

Comfort, dear mother. God is much displeas'd
That you take with unthankfulness his doing.
In common worldly things 'tis call'd ungrateful
With dull unwillingness to repay a debt
Which with a bounteous hand was kindly lent;
Much more to be thus opposite with heaven,
For it requires the royal debt it lent you.

Rivers

Madam, bethink you, like a careful mother,
Of the young prince your son. Send straight for him;
Let him be crown'd; in him your comfort lives.
Drown desperate sorrow in dead Edward's grave,
And plant your joys in living Edward's throne.

Enter GLOUCESTER, BUCKINGHAM, DERBY, HASTINGS, *and* RATCLIFF

Gloucester

Sister, have comfort. All of us have cause
To wail the dimming of our shining star;
But none can help our harms by wailing them.
Madam, my mother, I do cry you mercy;
I did not see your Grace. Humbly on my knee
I crave your blessing.

Duchess of York

God bless thee; and put meekness in thy breast,
Love, charity, obedience, and true duty!

Gloucester

Amen! [*Aside*] And make me die a good old man!
That is the butt end of a mother's blessing;
I marvel that her Grace did leave it out.

Buckingham

You cloudy princes and heart-sorrowing peers,
That bear this heavy mutual load of moan,
Now cheer each other in each other's love.
Though we have spent our harvest of this king,
We are to reap the harvest of his son.

117-19. Their hate for each other is compared to a septic wound that has swollen and burst, and then been dressed; it now needs time to heal. *rancour:* festering.

120. *Me seemeth:* it seems to me.
little train: few attendants.
121. *Ludlow:* a town near the Welsh border from which the prince had been ruling his Welsh territories.
fet: fetched.

124-5. 'Indeed, my lord, for fear that a large force might provoke the enemies, who have recently been made our friends, to take some action against him.'

127. *the estate:* the Yorkist rule.
green: inexperienced, weak.
ungovern'd: not used to governing.
128-9. 'When we are free to do what we like (to protect ourselves).'

132. *I hope:* I trust it's true that . . .
133. *compact:* agreement.

136. *breach:* breaking.
137. 'Which might be said if a large party went (to meet the prince).'

143. *Madam:* the Duchess of York.
144. *censures:* advice, opinions.

The broken rancour of your high-swol'n hearts,
But lately splinter'd, knit, and join'd together,
Must gently be preserv'd, cherish'd, and kept.
Me seemeth good that, with some little train,
Forthwith from Ludlow the young prince be fet
Hither to London, to be crown'd our King.

Rivers

Why with some little train, my Lord of Buckingham?

Buckingham

Marry, my lord, lest by a multitude
The new-heal'd wound of malice should break out,
Which would be so much the more dangerous
By how much the estate is green and yet ungovern'd;
Where every horse bears his commanding rein
And may direct his course as please himself,
As well the fear of harm as harm apparent,
In my opinion, ought to be prevented.

Gloucester

I hope the King made peace with all of us;
And the compact is firm and true in me.

Rivers

And so in me; and so, I think, in all.
Yet, since it is but green, it should be put
To no apparent likelihood of breach,
Which haply by much company might be urg'd;
Therefore I say with noble Buckingham
That it is meet so few should fetch the Prince.

Hastings

And so say I.

Gloucester

Then be it so; and go we to determine
Who they shall be that straight shall post to Ludlow.
Madam, and you, my sister, will you go
To give your censures in this business?

Exeunt all but BUCKINGHAM *and* GLOUCESTER

147. *by the way:* on the journey.
sort occasion: provide an opportunity.
148. *index:* In Elizabethan times this meant the table of contents at the beginning of a book; so, here it is equivalent to 'preface' or 'introduction.'
story . . . talk'd of: Buckingham is referring to a plan which he and Richard have recently made together.
150-3. This little episode shows the beginning of Buckingham's rise to become Richard's chief companion and assistant; but to our ears Richard's appreciation sounds unlikely to last. We cannot imagine that he would allow himself to be directed like a child by anybody.
150. *consistory:* place he gets all his good ideas from.

SCENE III

4. *seldom comes the better:* there are very few days when there is any good news.
5. *giddy:* unstable, a world in which people will not know what to expect.

Buckingham
My lord, whoever journeys to the Prince,
For God sake, let not us two stay at home;
For by the way I'll sort occasion,
As index to the story we late talk'd of,
To part the Queen's proud kindred from the Prince.

Gloucester
My other self, my counsel's consistory,
My oracle, my prophet, my dear cousin,
I, as a child, will go by thy direction.
Toward Ludlow then, for we'll not stay behind.

Exeunt

SCENE III—*London. A street*

Enter one CITIZEN *at one door, and* ANOTHER *at the other*

First Citizen
Good morrow, neighbour. Whither away so fast?

Second Citizen
I promise you, I scarcely know myself.
Hear you the news abroad?

First Citizen
Yes, that the King is dead.

Second Citizen
Ill news, by'r lady; seldom comes the better.
I fear, I fear 'twill prove a giddy world.

Enter another CITIZEN

Third Citizen
Neighbours, God speed!

First Citizen
Give you good morrow, sir.

Third Citizen
Doth the news hold of good King Edward's death?

Second Citizen
Ay, sir, it is too true; God help the while!

12-15. 'We can hope for good government in his reign. Until he is of age, his council may govern well; and when he is old enough to rule by himself, he may govern well.'

16. *So . . . state:* the kingdom then was just as it is now.

17. *but at:* when only.

18. *wot:* knows.

20. *politic:* wise.
grave: serious and well-informed.

25-6. 'For rivalry about who shall have most influence (over the new king) will cause trouble for us all.'

28. *haught:* proud, haughty.

29-30. 'If someone could rule them, instead of their ruling others, the kingdom, that is now so troubled, would be able to care for itself as it has done in the past.'

31. There was a proverbial saying, 'It is good to fear the worst.'

35. *Untimely:* coming at the wrong season.

Third Citizen
Then, masters, look to see a troublous world.

First Citizen
No, no; by God's good grace, his son shall reign.

Third Citizen
Woe to that land that's govern'd by a child.

Second Citizen
In him there is a hope of government,
Which, in his nonage, council under him,
And, in his full and ripened years, himself,
No doubt, shall then, and till then, govern well.

First Citizen
So stood the state when Henry the Sixth
Was crown'd in Paris but at nine months old.

Third Citizen
Stood the state so? No, no, good friends, God wot;
For then this land was famously enrich'd
With politic grave counsel; then the King
Had virtuous uncles to protect his Grace.

First Citizen
Why, so hath this, both by his father and mother.

Third Citizen
Better it were they all came by his father,
Or by his father there were none at all;
For emulation who shall now be nearest
Will touch us all too near, if God prevent not.
O, full of danger is the Duke of Gloucester!
And the Queen's sons and brothers haught and proud;
And were they to be rul'd, and not to rule,
This sickly land might solace as before.

First Citizen
Come, come, we fear the worst; all will be well.

Third Citizen
When clouds are seen, wise men put on their cloaks;
When great leaves fall, then winter is at hand;
When the sun sets, who doth not look for night?
Untimely storms make men expect a dearth.

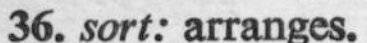

36. *sort:* arranges.

41. 'It is always like this before great changes happen.'

SCENE IV

Stage Direction. The Duke of York is Queen Elizabeth's younger son.

All may be well; but, if God sort it so,
'Tis more than we deserve or I expect.

Second Citizen

Truly, the hearts of men are full of fear.
You cannot reason almost with a man
That looks not heavily and full of dread.

Third Citizen

Before the days of change, still is it so;
By a divine instinct men's minds mistrust
Ensuing danger; as by proof we see
The water swell before a boist'rous storm.
But leave it all to God. Whither away?

Second Citizen

Marry, we were sent for to the justices.

Third Citizen

And so was I; I'll bear you company.

Exeunt

SCENE IV—*London. The palace*

Enter the ARCHBISHOP OF YORK, *the young* DUKE OF YORK, QUEEN ELIZABETH, *and the* DUCHESS OF YORK

Archbishop

Last night, I hear, they lay at Stony Stratford,
And at Northampton they do rest to-night;
To-morrow or next day they will be here.

Duchess of York

I long with all my heart to see the Prince.
I hope he is much grown since last I saw him.

Queen Elizabeth

But I hear no; they say my son of York
Has almost overta'en him in his growth.

York

Ay, mother; but I would not have it so.

16-17. *did not hold in him:* did not prove true of him.

21. The Archbishop seems to be trying to stop the queen from saying something she might regret, rather than to be rebuking her.

23. *if I . . . remember'd:* if I had thought of it.
24. *given . . . flout:* taunted my uncle.
25. *To touch:* about, referring to.

28. This would be taken as a sign of something strange and probably evil in the child; that is why the next few speeches try to hide where the story came from.

Duchess of York
Why, my good cousin, it is good to grow.
York
Grandam, one night as we did sit at supper,
My uncle Rivers talk'd how I did grow
More than my brother. 'Ay,' quoth my uncle Gloucester
'Small herbs have grace: great weeds do grow apace.'
And since, methinks, I would not grow so fast,
Because sweet flow'rs are slow and weeds make haste.
Duchess of York
Good faith, good faith, the saying did not hold
In him that did object the same to thee.
He was the wretched'st thing when he was young,
So long a-growing and so leisurely
That, if his rule were true, he should be gracious.
Archbishop
And so no doubt he is, my gracious madam.
Duchess of York
I hope he is; but yet let mothers doubt.
York
Now, by my troth, if I had been remember'd,
I could have given my uncle's Grace a flout
To touch his growth nearer than he touch'd mine.
Duchess of York
How, my young York? I prithee let me hear it.
York
Marry, they say my uncle grew so fast
That he could gnaw a crust at two hours old.
'Twas full two years ere I could get a tooth.
Grandam, this would have been a biting jest.
Duchess of York
I prithee, pretty York, who told thee this?
York
Grandam, his nurse.
Duchess of York
His nurse! Why she was dead ere thou wast born.

35. *parlous:* troublesome.
shrewd: clever, quick-witted.

37. 'Children hear more than they should.' A pitcher is a large jug with two handles. The queen seems to imply that York had heard the story from her.

41-3. Richard treated Prince Edward and his uncles at first with all proper courtesy when he met them; but after one night he arrested the uncles and took the prince into his custody, though still treating him with respect. Edward IV had, of course, appointed Richard Protector, and therefore guardian of the young king.
42. *Pomfret:* Pontefract, in Yorkshire, where they would be imprisoned and killed.

46. 'I have told you all I can tell you.'

50. *hind:* deer.
51. *jet:* encroach (i.e. threaten to take over). The word 'jet' is connected with 'jut'.
52. *innocent:* inexperienced.
aweless: not inspiring respect.

York
If 'twere not she, I cannot tell who told me.
Queen Elizabeth
A parlous boy! Go to, you are too shrewd.
Archbishop
Good madam, be not angry with the child.
Queen Elizabeth
Pitchers have ears.

Enter a MESSENGER

Archbishop
Here comes a messenger. What news?
Messenger
Such news, my lord, as grieves me to report.
Queen Elizabeth
How doth the Prince?
Messenger Well, madam, and in health.
Duchess of York
What is thy news?
Messenger Lord Rivers and Lord Grey
Are sent to Pomfret, and with them
Sir Thomas Vaughan, prisoners.
Duchess of York
Who hath committed them?
Messenger The mighty Dukes,
Gloucester and Buckingham.
Archbishop For what offence?
Messenger
The sum of all I can, I have disclos'd.
Why or for what the nobles were committed
Is all unknown to me, my gracious lord.
Queen Elizabeth
Ay me, I see the ruin of my house!
The tiger now hath seiz'd the gentle hind;
Insulting tyranny begins to jet
Upon the innocent and aweless throne.
Welcome, destruction, blood, and massacre!
I see, as in a map, the end of all.

55-65. The Duchess's speech sums up her feelings about the pointlessness of the continual political fighting, and prepares us to accept her reconciliation with her former enemy Queen Margaret, at a later stage.
55. *wrangling days:* days of argument and quarrelling.

60. *being seated:* having gained the throne.

60-1. *domestic . . . over-blown:* civil wars all ended.

63. *preposterous:* unnatural.

64. *frantic:* mad, crazy.
spleen: spitefulness.

66. The queen is going to seek safety in some religious house or institution.

71. *The seal I keep:* The Archbishop was Lord Chancellor, the chief lawyer in the kingdom. The stamp of the Great Seal was the king's way of showing that he had passed the law on which the seal was set. The Archbishop is hoping to stop anyone who is not approved of by Queen Elizabeth from ruling.
71-2. *so betide . . . yours!* Let me be treated by fortune according to the way I look after you and your family.

Duchess of York
Accursed and unquiet wrangling days,
How many of you have mine eyes beheld!
My husband lost his life to get the crown;
And often up and down my sons were toss'd
For me to joy and weep their gain and loss;
And being seated, and domestic broils
Clean over-blown, themselves the conquerors
Make war upon themselves—brother to brother,
Blood to blood, self against self. O, preposterous
And frantic outrage, end thy damned spleen,
Or let me die, to look on death no more!

Queen Elizabeth
Come, come, my boy; we will to sanctuary.
Madam, farewell.

Duchess of York Stay, I will go with you.

Queen Elizabeth
You have no cause.

Archbishop [*To the* QUEEN] My gracious lady, go.
And thither bear your treasure and your goods.
For my part, I'll resign unto your Grace
The seal I keep; and so betide to me
As well I tender you and all of yours!
Go, I'll conduct you to the sanctuary.

Exeunt

ACT THREE

SCENE I

The scene introduces the Prince of Wales. He and his brother are meant to be seen as attractive, lively youngsters, so that their murder will be as shocking as possible. Richard and Buckingham for various reasons find the boys irritating.

This episode also shows the growing importance of Buckingham as Richard's assistant. Although he is loyal and capable, he has a different approach from Richard's and is not as calm as Richard himself.

Stage Direction. Cardinal Bourchier was Archbishop of Canterbury.

1. *your chamber:* London was often so called when the king was in residence there.
4. *crosses:* troubles.
6. He is thinking of the members of his mother's family who have been arrested during the journey.

7-15. Richard doubtless enjoys the irony of this sermon on hypocrisy. Its truth is shown even as it is spoken.
7. *untainted:* unspoiled, still clean.

11. *jumpeth with:* truly represents.

16. *they were none:* they were not false.

17. The Lord Mayor represents the interests of the city and citizens of London. If Richard can get the citizens on his side he will have valuable support.

ACT THREE

SCENE I—*London. A street*

The trumpets sound. Enter the PRINCE OF WALES, GLOUCESTER, BUCKINGHAM, CATESBY, CARDINAL BOURCHIER, *and* OTHERS

Buckingham
Welcome, sweet Prince, to London, to your chamber.

Gloucester
Welcome, dear cousin, my thoughts' sovereign.
The weary way hath made you melancholy.

Prince
No, uncle; but our crosses on the way
Have made it tedious, wearisome, and heavy.
I want more uncles here to welcome me.

Gloucester
Sweet Prince, the untainted virtue of your years
Hath not yet div'd into the world's deceit;
Nor more can you distinguish of a man
Than of his outward show; which, God He knows,
Seldom or never jumpeth with the heart.
Those uncles which you want were dangerous;
Your Grace attended to their sugar'd words
But look'd not on the poison of their hearts.
God keep you from them and from such false friends!

Prince
God keep me from false friends! but they were none.

Gloucester
My lord, the Mayor of London comes to greet you.

Enter the LORD MAYOR *and his* TRAIN

21. *ere:* before.
us: i.e. me. Edward is speaking like a king.
22. *slug:* lazy, slow person.

26. *On what occasion:* for what reason.

28. *tender:* considerate.

30. *perforce:* by force.
withheld: stopped from coming.

31. *an indirect . . . course:* awkward and confusing behaviour. Buckingham's swearing is very mild, but it is strong enough to show that he is annoyed.

39. *anon:* at once.
obdurate: resisting obstinately.
41. It was understood that those who took refuge in a church were safe from everyone, even from legitimate authority.
44-56. The determination behind this argument is clear. Buckingham is working well for Richard. But his manner, his lawyer's way of juggling with words, is quite different from Richard's own way of dealing with things.
44. *senseless-obstinate:* Buckingham means that the cardinal is too content to stick to old ways without thinking out the reason for the actions.

Mayor

God bless your Grace with health and happy days!

Prince

I thank you, good my lord, and thank you all.
I thought my mother and my brother York
Would long ere this have met us on the way.
Fie, what a slug is Hastings, that he comes not
To tell us whether they will come or no!

Enter LORD HASTINGS

Buckingham

And, in good time, here comes the sweating lord.

Prince

Welcome, my lord. What, will our mother come?

Hastings

On what occasion, God He knows, not I,
The Queen your mother and your brother York
Have taken sanctuary. The tender Prince
Would fain have come with me to meet your Grace,
But by his mother was perforce withheld.

Buckingham

Fie, what an indirect and peevish course
Is this of hers? Lord Cardinal, will your Grace
Persuade the Queen to send the Duke of York
Unto his princely brother presently?
If she deny, Lord Hastings, go with him
And from her jealous arms pluck him perforce.

Cardinal Bourchier

My Lord of Buckingham, if my weak oratory
Can from his mother win the Duke of York,
Anon expect him here; but if she be obdurate
To mild entreaties, God in heaven forbid
We should infringe the holy privilege
Of blessed sanctuary! Not for all this land
Would I be guilty of so deep a sin.

Buckingham

You are too senseless-obstinate, my lord,

45. *Too . . . traditional:* paying too much respect to old customs.

46. 'If you look at the question less strictly, as people do these days . . .'

50. *wit:* intelligence, sense.

53. *thence:* that place there.

54. 'You are not taking away anybody's rights by doing this.'

62. *sojourn:* live.

66. *and shall be thought most fit:* and wherever shall be considered most suitable.

68. 'I like the Tower least of all places.'

69. *Julius Caesar:* a Roman general and later ruler of Rome. He conquered western Europe and invaded Britain, but he did not, in fact, build the Tower of London.

71. *re-edified:* rebuilt.

Too ceremonious and traditional.
Weigh it but with the grossness of this age,
You break not sanctuary in seizing him.
The benefit thereof is always granted
To those whose dealings have deserv'd the place
And those who have the wit to claim the place.
This Prince hath neither claim'd it nor deserv'd it,
And therefore, in mine opinion, cannot have it.
Then, taking him from thence that is not there,
You break no privilege nor charter there.
Oft have I heard of sanctuary men;
But sanctuary children never till now.

Cardinal Bourchier

My lord, you shall overrule my mind for once.
Come on, Lord Hastings, will you go with me?

Hastings

I go, my lord.

Prince

Good lords, make all the speedy haste you may.

Exeunt CARDINAL *and* HASTINGS

Say, uncle Gloucester, if our brother come,
Where shall we sojourn till our coronation?

Gloucester

Where it seems best unto your royal self.
If I may counsel you, some day or two
Your Highness shall repose you at the Tower,
Then where you please and shall be thought most fit
For your best health and recreation.

Prince

I do not like the Tower, of any place.
Did Julius Caesar build that place, my lord?

Buckingham

He did, my gracious lord, begin that place,
Which, since, succeeding ages have re-edified.

Prince

Is it upon record, or else reported

75. 'But even, my Lord, if it were not written down . . .'

77. *posterity:* people who live later.

78. *general . . . day:* the day on which the world will end.

79. Richard is referring to a proverb: 'Those who are wise when young do not live long.' The 'story' mentioned by Buckingham in Act II, Scene ii is beginning to be told. Richard's remark shows him amusing himself with the thought that the princes' death is almost decided by fate, and so he, Richard, is hardly to blame for it.

81. *without characters:* without being written down.

82. *formal vice, Iniquity:* The Duchess of York has already referred to vice in this sense: a comically evil character in the old Morality plays. Iniquity was another name for him. He was a stock character, appearing in many plays, not made into an individual person.

83. 'I suggest two meanings for one phrase.' Richard's words are ironical for the princes' fame does live long, because of Richard's treatment of them.

85-6. 'The deeds he performed because he was brave stimulated his imagination, and gave him something to think about; which he then wrote down so that his brave deeds would be remembered.'

90. What do you think Buckingham's attitude is at this point? Is he bored; pretending to be interested; sarcastic even?

91-3. Thinking of Caesar's conquests has given the prince this idea. During the reign of Henry VI all but a very few of the English territories in France had been lost.

91. *An if:* if.

94. 'When the spring comes early, summer does not last long.' In other words, being such a clever youth, Edward will not live long as a man.

96. *our loving brother:* Edward refers to Richard of York himself.

Successively from age to age, he built it?

Buckingham

Upon record, my gracious lord.

Prince

But say, my lord, it were not register'd,
Methinks the truth should live from age to age,
As 'twere retail'd to all posterity,
Even to the general all-ending day.

Gloucester [*Aside*]

So wise so young, they say, do never live long.

Prince

What say you, uncle?

Gloucester

I say, without characters, fame lives long.
[*Aside*] Thus, like the formal vice, Iniquity,
I moralize two meanings in one word.

Prince

That Julius Caesar was a famous man;
With what his valour did enrich his wit,
His wit set down to make his valour live.
Death makes no conquest of this conqueror;
For now he lives in fame, though not in life.
I'll tell you what, my cousin Buckingham—

Buckingham

What, my gracious lord?

Prince

An if I live until I be a man,
I'll win our ancient right in France again,
Or die a soldier as I liv'd a king.

Gloucester [*Aside*]

Short summers lightly have a forward spring.

Enter young YORK, HASTINGS, *and the* CARDINAL

Buckingham

Now, in good time, here comes the Duke of York.

Prince

Richard of York, how fares our loving brother?

98. *to our grief:* He is sad because the cause of his being king is their father's death.
99. *Too late:* very recently.

106. *I . . . so:* He must, of course, show respect to the king.

107. *beholding:* obliged.

109. *kinsman:* relative.

110. York is testing Richard to see whether he means what he says.

111. Two meanings here: (1) I will gladly give you my dagger as present; (2) I will gladly kill you with my dagger.

112. The prince is teasing him, or criticizing him for asking for a gi

113-14. '(I am begging) from my kind uncle, who, I know, will give it me anyway; and I am asking only for a little, unimportant thin that it will not hurt him to give me.'

117. *light:* A man's sword would be too heavy for a boy; but in Yor reply, 'light' means unimportant as well as of the right weight.

York
Well my dread lord; so must I call you now.
Prince
Ay brother, to our grief, as it is yours.
Too late he died that might have kept that title,
Which by his death hath lost much majesty.
Gloucester
How fares our cousin, noble Lord of York?
York
I thank you, gentle uncle. O, my lord,
You said that idle weeds are fast in growth.
The Prince my brother hath outgrown me far.
Gloucester
He hath, my lord.
York And therefore is he idle?
Gloucester
O, my fair cousin, I must not say so.
York
Then he is more beholding to you than I.
Gloucester
He may command me as my sovereign;
But you have power in me as in a kinsman.
York
I pray you, uncle, give me this dagger.
Gloucester
My dagger, little cousin? With all my heart!
Prince
A beggar, brother?
York
Of my kind uncle, that I know will give,
And being but a toy, which is no grief to give.
Gloucester
A greater gift than that I'll give my cousin.
York
A greater gift! O, that's the sword to it!
Gloucester
Ay, gentle cousin, were it light enough.

119. *weightier:* more important, more valuable.

121. 'I wouldn't think much of it even if it were heavier.' *heavier:* bigger, more impressive.

125. York would not appear to be very grateful. In this way he would be paying back Richard for not wanting to give him the present.

126. *will . . . talk:* always gives quick, clever answers.

127. *to bear with:* to put up with, to tolerate.

128. *bear:* carry.

131. York is making fun of Richard's hunch-back. People who had performing apes used to have a saddle on their shoulders to carry the apes on. How do you imagine that an actor taking Richard's part would react to the boy's remark?

132-5. Buckingham's supposed admiration contains a threat that will be missed by all except Richard. Perhaps some of these lines are spoken aside to Richard and are flattery of him.

132. *sharp-provided:* full of clever ideas.

133. *mitigate:* temper, lessen.

141. *Lord Protector:* Richard, Duke of Gloucester.

York
O, then, I see you will part but with light gifts:
In weightier things you'll say a beggar nay.

Gloucester
It is too heavy for your Grace to wear.

York
I weigh it lightly, were it heavier.

Gloucester
What, would you have my weapon, little lord?

York
I would, that I might thank you as you call me.

Gloucester
How?

York
Little.

Prince
My Lord of York will still be cross in talk.
Uncle, your Grace knows how to bear with him.

York
You mean, to bear me, not to bear with me,
Uncle, my brother mocks both you and me;
Because that I am little, like an ape,
He thinks that you should bear me on your shoulders.

Buckingham
With what a sharp-provided wit he reasons!
To mitigate the scorn he gives his uncle
He prettily and aptly taunts himself.
So cunning and so young is wonderful.

Gloucester
My lord, will't please you pass along?
Myself and my good cousin Buckingham
Will to your mother, to entreat of her
To meet you at the Tower and welcome you.

York
What, will you go unto the Tower, my lord?

Prince
My Lord Protector needs will have it so.

142. *I shall . . . quiet:* I shall have disturbed sleep.

145. *grandam:* grandmother, i.e. the Duchess of York.

148. *fear:* He means fear that they will come to some harm.
149. *my Lord:* Lord Hastings.

Stage Direction. A sennet was a fanfare of trumpets on a ceremonia stage entrance or exit. Catesby was at one time a close associate o Hastings.

151. *prating:* chattering.
152. *incensed:* encouraged, put up to it.
153. *opprobriously:* shamefully.

154. *perilous:* advanced for his age, and difficult.
155. *forward:* precocious, advanced for his age.
156. 'Everything about him is just like his mother.'

157. *let them rest:* don't bother about them any more. They are, o course, going to be dealt with.
158-9. 'You have sworn a binding oath both to carry out our plan an also to keep to yourself what we tell you.'

163. *instalment:* installation (i.e. putting him on the throne).
this noble Duke: Richard.

165. *He:* Hastings.
his father's sake: King Edward IV's sake.

York
I shall not sleep in quiet at the Tower.
Gloucester
Why, what should you fear?
York
Marry, my uncle Clarence' angry ghost.
My grandam told me he was murder'd there.
Prince
I fear no uncles dead.
Gloucester
Nor none that live, I hope.
Prince
An if they live, I hope I need not fear.
But come, my lord; and with a heavy heart,
Thinking on them, go I unto the Tower.

A sennet. Exeunt all but GLOUCESTER, BUCKINGHAM, *and* CATESBY

Buckingham
Think you, my lord, this little prating York
Was not incensed by his subtle mother
To taunt and scorn you thus opprobriously?
Gloucester
No doubt, no doubt. O, 'tis a perilous boy;
Bold, quick, ingenious, forward, capable.
He is all the mother's, from the top to toe.
Buckingham
Well, let them rest. Come hither, Catesby.
Thou art sworn as deeply to effect what we intend
As closely to conceal what we impart.
Thou know'st our reasons urg'd upon the way.
What think'st thou? Is it not an easy matter
To make William Lord Hastings of our mind,
For the instalment of this noble Duke
In the seat royal of this famous isle?
Catesby
He for his father's sake so loves the Prince

166. *aught:* anything.

170. *as . . . far off:* without giving anything away, indirectly.
sound: test (his opinion).
171. 'What his attitude to our plan is'.

173. *sit about:* meet to discuss.

174. *tractable to us:* likely to come on our side.

176. *leaden:* slow to respond.
icy: unsympathetic and uninterested.

179. *divided councils:* The Privy Council, the committee which advised the king, was to split into two groups which were to meet in different places.

181-5. Richard appears to want Hastings on his side to save himself trouble; so he is making sure that Hastings knows who is winning in the struggle for power between Richard and the queen's family. But there is still perhaps a sneering threat in the reference to Mistress Shore. Incidentally, Lord Rivers seems to have been another of Mistress Shore's lovers.
181. *Lord William:* Lord Hastings.

187. *with . . . heed:* taking care to do just what you have told me.

190. *Crosby House:* Richard's palace in London.

That he will not be won to aught against him.

Buckingham

What think'st thou then of Stanley? Will not he?

Catesby

He will do all in all as Hastings doth.

Buckingham

Well then, no more but this: go, gentle Catesby,
And, as it were far off, sound thou Lord Hastings
How he doth stand affected to our purpose;
And summon him to-morrow to the Tower,
To sit about the coronation.
If thou dost find him tractable to us,
Encourage him, and tell him all our reasons;
If he be leaden, icy, cold, unwilling,
Be thou so too, and so break off the talk,
And give us notice of his inclination;
For we to-morrow hold divided councils,
Wherein thyself shalt highly be employ'd.

Gloucester

Commend me to Lord William. Tell him, Catesby,
His ancient knot of dangerous adversaries
To-morrow are let blood at Pomfret Castle;
And bid my lord, for joy of this good news,
Give Mistress Shore one gentle kiss the more.

Buckingham

Good Catesby, go effect this business soundly.

Catesby

My good lords both, with all the heed I can.

Gloucester

Shall we hear from you, Catesby, ere we sleep?

Catesby

You shall, my lord.

Gloucester

At Crosby House, there shall you find us both.

Exit CATESBY

191-2. Buckingham is not yet the same cool villain that Richard is. He still worries.

193. *something . . . determine:* we will decide later on an explanation of why we have killed him.
194. *look when:* as soon as.
195. *movables:* portable property such as treasures, furnishings, furniture.

197. *that promise:* See Act IV, Scene ii, line 92 for what happens when Buckingham does claim what Richard here promises.

198. *look:* expect.

199. *betimes:* early.

200. 'We can put our various schemes into some order.'

SCENE II

2. *Within:* off-stage, as though coming from inside the house.

6. *tedious:* Nights are, naturally, tedious to someone who cannot sleep.

Buckingham
Now, my lord, what shall we do if we perceive
Lord Hastings will not yield to our complots?

Gloucester
Chop off his head—something we will determine.
And, look when I am King, claim thou of me
The earldom of Hereford and all the movables
Whereof the King my brother was possess'd.

Buckingham
I'll claim that promise at your Grace's hand.

Gloucester
And look to have it yielded with all kindness.
Come, let us sup betimes, that afterwards
We may digest our complots in some form.

Exeunt

SCENE II—*Before Lord Hastings' house*

Enter a MESSENGER *to the door of* HASTINGS

Messenger
My lord, my lord!

Knocking

Hastings [*Within*]
Who knocks?

Messenger
One from the Lord Stanley.

Hastings [*Within*]
What is't o'clock?

Messenger
Upon the stroke of four.

Enter LORD HASTINGS

Hastings
Cannot my Lord Stanley sleep these tedious nights?

10. *certifies:* sends word that it is certain.

11. *boar:* another reference to Richard's emblem, a white boar.
razed off: torn off. In other words, Richard had attacked and defeated Stanley. Perhaps the plucking off of the helmet signified his execution.
13. *that . . . determin'd:* something may be decided.
14. *rue:* be sorry for.

16. *presently:* at once.

17. *post:* ride as quickly as possible.

18. *divines:* foresees by intuition.

22. *my good friend Catesby:* How little of a 'good friend' Catesby is to Hastings is obvious in the previous scene.
23. *toucheth:* concerns.
24. *intelligence:* information.
25. *shallow:* unimportant.
instance: supporting evidence.

29. *incense:* provoke.

Messenger

So it appears by that I have to say.
First, he commends him to your noble self.

Hastings

What then?

Messenger

Then certifies your lordship that this night
He dreamt the boar had razed off his helm.
Besides, he says there are two councils kept,
And that may be determin'd at the one
Which may make you and him to rue at th' other.
Therefore he sends to know your lordship's pleasure—
If you will presently take horse with him
And with all speed post with him toward the north
To shun the danger that his soul divines.

Hastings

Go, fellow, go, return unto thy lord;
Bid him not fear the separated council:
His honour and myself are at the one,
And at the other is my good friend Catesby;
Where nothing can proceed that toucheth us
Whereof I shall not have intelligence.
Tell him his fears are shallow, without instance;
And for his dreams, I wonder he's so simple
To trust the mock'ry of unquiet slumbers.
To fly the boar before the boar pursues
Were to incense the boar to follow us
And make pursuit where he did mean no chase.
Go, bid thy master rise and come to me;
And we will both together to the Tower,
Where, he shall see, the boar will use us kindly.

Messenger

I'll go, my lord, and tell him what you say.

Exit

Enter CATESBY

37. *tott'ring state:* a modern equivalent might be 'unstable kingdom'.

38. *reeling:* This word and 'tott'ring' both suggest the movements of a drunken man. The metaphors imply that no-one is governing the country.
40. *garland:* link or loop of flowers worn as a decoration.

41. There can be no doubt about Hastings' attitude: he is deeply shocked.

43. *crown:* here means head.

47. *gain:* winning.

52. *still:* always.

54. *in true descent:* lawful, by right of heredity.
55. 'I will refuse to do t, even f it costs me my life.'

58-9. The sentence is clumsy but the meaning is clear. He is talking about Rivers and Grey now.
58. *my master's:* King Edward IV's.

61. *send some packing:* send some to their deaths.

Catesby
Many good morrows to my noble lord!

Hastings
Good morrow, Catesby; you are early stirring.
What news, what news, in this our tott'ring state?

Catesby
It is a reeling world indeed, my lord;
And I believe will never stand upright
Till Richard wear the garland of the realm.

Hastings
How, wear the garland! Dost thou mean the crown?

Catesby
Ay, my good lord.

Hastings
I'll have this crown of mine cut from my shoulders
Before I'll see the crown so foul misplac'd.
But canst thou guess that he doth aim at it?

Catesby
Ay, on my life; and hopes to find you forward
Upon his party for the gain thereof;
And thereupon he sends you this good news,
That this same very day your enemies,
The kindred of the Queen, must die at Pomfret.

Hastings
Indeed, I am no mourner for that news,
Because they have been still my adversaries;
But that I'll give my voice on Richard's side
To bar my master's heirs in true descent,
God knows I will not do it to the death.

Catesby
God keep your lordship in that gracious mind!

Hastings
But I shall laugh at this a twelve month hence,
That they which brought me in my master's hate,
I live to look upon their tragedy.
Well, Catesby, ere a fortnight make me older,
I'll send some packing that yet think not on't.

62-3. Catesby is apparently referring to the enemies of Hastings, but is perhaps trying to warn Hastings to think again. The irony continues in the reply.

69. *make . . . account of:* think highly of.

70. The severed heads of traitors were stuck on poles at the entrance to London Bridge.

72. Hastings is in such a good humour that he jokes with Stanley about his fears.

73. *unprovided:* without the necessary weapons.

76. *several:* separate.

80. *but that . . . secure:* if I did not know that our position is quite safe . ..

83. *jocund:* cheerful.

84. *mistrust:* doubt, be afraid.

85. *o'ercast:* became cloudy. He is comparing good fortune to bright, sunny weather, and bad fortune to cloudy, stormy weather.

86. *stab of rancour:* act of hatred. He is thinking of the arrest of the queen's relatives. Stanley does not yet know that they are going to be executed.

88. *The day is spent:* It is getting late.

Catesby

'Tis a vile thing to die, my gracious lord,
When men are unprepar'd and look not for it.

Hastings

O monstrous, monstrous! And so falls it out
With Rivers, Vaughan, Grey; and so 'twill do
With some men else that think themselves as safe
As thou and I, who, as thou knowest, are dear
To princely Richard and to Buckingham.

Catesby

The Princes both make high account of you—
[*Aside*] For they account his head upon the bridge.

Hastings

I know they do, and I have well deserv'd it.

Enter LORD STANLEY

Come on, come on; where is your boar-spear, man?
Fear you the boar, and go so unprovided?

Stanley

My lord, good morrow; good morrow, Catesby.
You may jest on, but, by the holy rood,
I do not like these several councils, I.

Hastings

My lord, I hold my life as dear as yours,
And never in my days, I do protest,
Was it so precious to me as 'tis now.
Think you, but that I know our state secure,
I would be so triumphant as I am?

Stanley

The lords at Pomfret, when they rode from London,
Were jocund and suppos'd their states were sure,
And they indeed had no cause to mistrust;
But yet you see how soon the day o'ercast.
This sudden stab of rancour I misdoubt;
Pray God, I say, I prove a needless coward.
What, shall we toward the Tower? The day is spent.

89. *have with you:* let's go, then.
Wot: know.

91-2. 'Because they were faithful men, they deserve to live more than some of their accusers deserve the important positions they hold.'

Stage Direction. It is an odd historical fact that the officer who accompanied Lord Hastings to the Tower himself bore the name of Hastings. In the Folio edition the pursuivant has no name, and Shakespeare probably preferred not to introduce such an irrelevant coincidence.

104. 'May God keep it so; so that you, your honour, may continue to be happy.'

105. *drink that:* Hastings is giving him a tip. (Compare the French word for a tip, 'pourboire').

Hastings
Come, come, have with you. Wot you what, my lord?
To-day the lords you talk'd of are beheaded.

Stanley
They, for their truth, might better wear their heads
Than some that have accus'd them wear their hats.
But come, my lord, let's away.

Enter HASTINGS, *a pursuivant*

Hastings
Go on before; I'll talk with this good fellow.

Exeunt STANLEY *and* CATESBY

How now, Hastings! How goes the world with thee?

Pursuivant
The better that your lordship please to ask.

Hastings
I tell thee, man, 'tis better with me now
Than when thou met'st me last where now we meet:
Then was I going prisoner to the Tower
By the suggestion of the Queen's allies;
But now, I tell thee—keep it to thyself—
This day those enemies are put to death,
And I in better state than e'er I was.

Pursuivant
God hold it, to your honour's good content!

Hastings
Gramercy, Hastings; there, drink that for me.

Throws him his purse

Pursuivant
I thank your honour.

Exit

Enter a PRIEST

Priest
Well met, my lord; I am glad to see your honour.

108. *Sir John:* Sir was a usual way of addressing a priest.

109. *exercise:* sermon.

110. *content:* reward.

Stage Direction. Hastings presumably promises a gift.

111. *wait upon:* visit.

114. *shriving work:* work that carries a risk with it so that a Christian would wish to confess his sins before he undertook it, just in case he died while doing it.

115. *Good faith:* You are quite right.

117. *go you . . . Tower?* One of the meetings of the council was in the Tower.

119. *thence:* from there.

121. Buckingham means that Hastings will have his last meal there; or simply that he will be there longer than he expects.

122. *wait upon:* go with.

SCENE III

Stage Direction. *carrying:* taking.

Hastings
I thank thee, good Sir John, with all my heart.
I am in your debt for your last exercise;
Come the next Sabbath, and I will content you.

He whispers in his ear

Priest
I'll wait upon your lordship.

Enter BUCKINGHAM

Buckingham
What, talking with a priest, Lord Chamberlain!
Your friends at Pomfret, they do need the priest:
Your honour hath no shriving work in hand.

Hastings
Good faith, and when I met this holy man,
The men you talk of came into my mind.
What, go you toward the Tower?

Buckingham
I do, my lord, but long I cannot stay there;
I shall return before your lordship thence.

Hastings
Nay, like enough, for I stay dinner there.

Buckingham [*Aside*]
And supper too, although thou knowest it not.—
Come, will you go?

Hastings I'll wait upon your lordship.

Exeunt

SCENE III—*Pomfret Castle*

Enter SIR RICHARD RATCLIFF, *with* HALBERDS, *carrying the Nobles,* RIVERS, GREY *and* VAUGHAN, *to death*

Rivers
Sir Richard Ratcliff, let me tell thee this:
To-day shalt thou behold a subject die

4. *from all:* and protect him from all.

5. *knot:* gang.

6. *cry woe:* be made to suffer.
hereafter: in the future.

7. *Dispatch:* hurry up.

10. *closure:* enclosure, fence.

12. *seat:* structure; a word used for a building as a whole.

14. *Margaret's curse:* The curse is in Act I, Scene iii, in the lines following 196; in particular, *God, I pray him, That none of you may live his natural age.* (lines 211-12).

21. *true:* loyal.

23. *is expiate:* has now come, is waiting to be.

For truth, for duty, and for loyalty.

Grey

God bless the Prince from all the pack of you!
A knot you are of damned blood-suckers.

Vaughan

You live that shall cry woe for this hereafter.

Ratcliff

Dispatch; the limit of your lives is out.

Rivers

O Pomfret, Pomfret! O thou bloody prison,
Fatal and ominous to noble peers!
Within the guilty closure of thy walls
Richard the Second here was hack'd to death;
And, for more slander to thy dismal seat,
We give to thee our guiltless blood to drink.

Grey

Now Margaret's curse is fall'n upon our heads,
When she exclaim'd on Hastings, you, and I,
For standing by when Richard stabb'd her son.

Rivers

Then curs'd she Richard, then curs'd she Buckingham,
Then curs'd she Hastings. O, remember, God,
To hear her prayer for them, as now for us!
And for my sister, and her princely sons,
Be satisfied, dear God, with our true blood,
Which, as thou know'st, unjustly must be spilt.

Ratcliff

Make haste; the hour of death is expiate.

Rivers

Come, Grey; come, Vaughan; let us here embrace.
Farewell, until we meet again in heaven.

Exeunt

SCENE IV

Stage Direction. Remember that Derby is Lord Stanley.

2. *determine of:* make up our minds about.
the coronation: i.e. of Edward V.

5. *wants but nomination:* only has to be named.

8. *inward with:* in the confidence of.

9. *soonest:* be most likely to.

10-12. Buckingham may or may not realize the irony of what he says; but his part in Richard's plot against Hastings ought to make him aware how foolish his comment might be.

19. 'I'll vote in place of the Duke.'

20. *he'll take . . . part:* He'll accept as a kindness on my part.

SCENE IV—*London. The Tower*

Enter BUCKINGHAM, DERBY, HASTINGS, *the* BISHOP OF ELY, RATCLIFF, LOVEL, *with* OTHERS *and seat themselves at a table*

Hastings
Now, noble peers, the cause why we are met
Is to determine of the coronation.
In God's name speak—when is the royal day?

Buckingham
Is all things ready for the royal time?

Derby
It is, and wants but nomination.

Bishop of Ely
To-morrow then I judge a happy day.

Buckingham
Who knows the Lord Protector's mind herein?
Who is most inward with the noble Duke?

Bishop of Ely
Your Grace, we think, should soonest know his mind.

Buckingham
We know each other's faces; for our hearts,
He knows no more of mine than I of yours;
Or I of his, my lord, than you of mine.
Lord Hastings, you and he are near in love.

Hastings
I thank his Grace, I know he loves me well;
But for his purpose in the coronation
I have not sounded him, nor he deliver'd
His gracious pleasure any way therein.
But you, my honourable lords, may name the time;
And in the Duke's behalf I'll give my voice,
Which, I presume, he'll take in gentle part.

Enter GLOUCESTER

31-3. By this discussion Richard gets away from the subject of the coronation, and also continues to play the part of a cheerful, friendly fellow.

37. *testy:* short-tempered, irritable.
so hot: so excitable and rash (in speaking up against Richard's suggestion).
39. *worshipfully:* respectfully.

Bishop of Ely
In happy time, here comes the Duke himself.

Gloucester
My noble lords and cousins all, good morrow.
I have been long a sleeper, but I trust
My absence doth neglect no great design
Which by my presence might have been concluded.

Buckingham
Had you not come upon your cue, my lord,
William Lord Hastings had pronounc'd your part—
I mean, your voice for crowning of the King.

Gloucester
Than my Lord Hastings no man might be bolder;
His lordship knows me well and loves me well.
My lord of Ely, when I was last in Holborn
I saw good strawberries in your garden there.
I do beseech you send for some of them.

Bishop of Ely
Marry and will, my lord, with all my heart.

Exit

Gloucester
Cousin of Buckingham, a word with you.

Takes him aside

Catesby hath sounded Hastings in our business,
And finds the testy gentleman so hot
That he will lose his head ere give consent
His master's child, as worshipfully he terms it,
Shall lose the royalty of England's throne.

Buckingham
Withdraw yourself awhile; I'll go with you.

Exeunt GLOUCESTER *and* BUCKINGHAM

Derby
We have not yet set down this day of triumph.
To-morrow, in my judgment, is too sudden;

44. *provided:* prepared.

45. *prolong'd:* postponed.

48. *smooth:* in a good mood.

49. *conceit:* idea in his head.

51-3. All those for whom Richard does not openly show enmity—as he does for the queen's family—must have felt like this about Richard, but the fact that Hastings says so makes him seem particularly weak in this dangerous game of politics.

51. *Christendom:* the parts of the world that are Christian.

54. Derby is much less sure that Hastings is right. He seems to be scornful of Hastings' simplicity. Perhaps he is partly getting his own back because Hastings did not take his dream seriously.

55. *livelihood:* cheerfulness.

58. Richard's mood has completely changed so that it contrasts terribly with his earlier manner and with Hastings' last remark.

63. *most forward:* the first to speak.

64. *doom:* condemn.

67-8. Since Richard's deformities were well-known, his suggestion here is another example of his impudence that shows us how strong he is. Only the simple, honest Hastings will speak out against him.

For I myself am not so well provided
As else I would be, were the day prolong'd.

Re-enter the BISHOP OF ELY

Bishop of Ely
Where is my lord the Duke of Gloucester?
I have sent for these strawberries.

Hastings
His Grace looks cheerfully and smooth this morning;
There's some conceit or other likes him well
When that he bids good morrow with such spirit.
I think there's never a man in Christendom
Can lesser hide his love or hate than he;
For by his face straight shall you know his heart.

Derby
What of his heart perceive you in his face
By any livelihood he show'd to-day?

Hastings
Marry, that with no man here he is offended;
For, were he, he had shown it in his looks.

Re-enter GLOUCESTER *and* BUCKINGHAM

Gloucester
I pray you all, tell me what they deserve
That do conspire my death with devilish plots
Of damned witchcraft, and that have prevail'd
Upon my body with their hellish charms?

Hastings
The tender love I bear your Grace, my lord,
Makes me most forward in this princely presence
To doom th' offenders, whosoe'er they be.
I say, my lord, they have deserved death.

Gloucester
Then be your eyes the witness of their evil.
Look how I am bewitch'd; behold, mine arm
Is like a blasted sapling wither'd up.
And this is Edward's wife, that monstrous witch,

70. *consorted:* associated for evil purposes.
harlot and *strumpet* both mean prostitute. Richard mentions Jane Shore only to catch Hastings, who duly allows himself to be trapped.

73-8. Richard, in his assumed rage, sweeps through the accusing, judging, and sentencing of Hastings, and then forces the rest to show whose side they are on; all without allowing anyone time to think.
73. *protector:* the man who maintains her with money.

79-86. Hastings' comments are the usual ones in the circumstances, in a play. The warnings of disaster, the realization of foolish pride, the moralizing about the worthlessness of worldly success, and the forecasting of disaster to the country are all found at other places in this play. Hastings' comments therefore remind us of several of the play's themes.
79. *whit:* very small quantity.
80. *too fond:* although I was too foolish to do so.
83. *foot-cloth:* A foot-cloth was a covering laid over the back of a horse. It was usually decorated with rich embroidery and hung down to the ground.
84. *started:* was startled and moved suddenly.
85. *loath:* reluctant.

91. *thy heavy curse:* See Act I, Scene iii, lines 210-14.

92. *lighted:* settled.

93. Ratcliff is again hurrying a man to his death. Is this because he is callous or because he is distressed and afraid?
would be at: wants to get on with.
94. *shrift:* confession.

97. 'The man who bases his hopes on the flimsy foundations (no firmer than air) of other people's friendly looks . . .'
99-100. Just as the drunken sailor is drowsy and likely to fall, so Hastings has not kept his eyes open to see what dangers threaten him.

Consorted with that harlot strumpet Shore,
That by their witchcraft thus have marked me.

Hastings

If they have done this deed, my noble lord—

Gloucester

If?—thou protector of this damned strumpet,
Talk'st thou to me of ifs? Thou art a traitor.
Off with his head! Now by Saint Paul I swear
I will not dine until I see the same.
Lovel and Ratcliff, look that it be done.
The rest that love me, rise and follow me.

Exeunt all but HASTINGS, LOVEL, *and* RATCLIFF

Hastings

Woe, woe, for England! not a whit for me;
For I, too fond, might have prevented this.
Stanley did dream the boar did raze our helms,
And I did scorn it and disdain to fly.
Three times to-day my foot-cloth horse did stumble,
And started when he look'd upon the Tower,
As loath to bear me to the slaughter-house.
O, now I need the priest that spake to me!
I now repent I told the pursuivant,
As too triumphing, how mine enemies
To-day at Pomfret bloodily were butcher'd,
And I myself secure in grace and favour.
O Margaret, Margaret, now thy heavy curse
Is lighted on poor Hastings' wretched head!

Ratcliff

Come, come, dispatch; the Duke would be at dinner.
Make a short shrift; he longs to see your head.

Hastings

O momentary grace of mortal men,
Which we more hunt for than the grace of God!
Who builds his hope in air of your good looks
Lives like a drunken sailor on a mast,
Ready with every nod to tumble down

100. *bowels:* deep parts.
deep: sea.

102. *bloody:* murderous.

104. 'That has ever been seen, even in the worst periods of history.'
105. *block:* A man who was to be decapitated put his head and neck on a block.

SCENE V

After the ruthless determination of the previous scene we find now a grim comedy—though no less determination—in the next stage o Richard's progress to the crown. Having got rid of Hastings, Richar now has to persuade the citizens of London to support him. For thei benefit he puts on two performances: the first, here, as the ever watchful guardian of the state; the second, in Act III, Scene vii, as th holy man who does not really want to have anything to do wit worldly affairs. We know from Richard's conversations with Bucking ham (lines 73-89) how vitally important he thinks public approval to him.

Stage Direction. Buckingham and Richard are at first on the walls the Tower, which would probably be represented by a gallery abov the stage. They speak to the others who are at ground level.
marvellous ill-favoured: of remarkably shabby appearance.

1. *quake:* tremble, shake.
2. *Murder:* cut off.
5. 'I can behave like a tragic actor using all his skill.' (Or, perhaps, 'ham' actor, a term used to describe a bad actor).
6. *pry:* peer, look closely.
7. *wagging of a straw:* an insignificant event.
8. *Intending:* pretending.
10. *ready . . . offices:* just waiting to do what they are meant to d
11. *to grace:* to help and make better.
stratagems: tricks.

14-20. The bustle here to be well defended and prepared for an atta is part of Richard's pretence that the country is in immediate dang because of Hastings' treachery.

Into the fatal bowels of the deep.

ovel

Come, come, dispatch; 'tis bootless to exclaim.

Iastings

O bloody Richard! Miserable England!
I prophesy the fearfull'st time to thee
That ever wretched age hath look'd upon.
Come, lead me to the block; bear him my head.
They smile at me who shortly shall be dead.

Exeunt

ENE V—*London. The Tower-walls*

Enter GLOUCESTER *and* BUCKINGHAM *in rotten armour, marvellous ill-favoured*

oucester

Come, cousin, canst thou quake and change thy colour,
Murder thy breath in middle of a word,
And then again begin, and stop again,
As if thou were distraught and mad with terror?

ckingham

Tut, I can counterfeit the deep tragedian;
Speak and look back, and pry on every side,
Tremble and start at wagging of a straw,
Intending deep suspicion. Ghastly looks
Are at my service, like enforced smiles;
And both are ready in their offices
At any time to grace my stratagems.
But what, is Catesby gone?

ucester

He is; and, see, he brings the mayor along.

Enter the LORD MAYOR *and* CATESBY

ckingham

Lord Mayor—

17. *o'erlook:* inspect.

23. *unsuspected:* How could he be anything else!

24. Richard's performance is, of course, put on for the Lord May

27-8. 'I told him everything, all my secrets.'

29. Hastings is compared to someone putting a mask of make-up his face; *smooth* suggests that he was innocent. The whole line mea 'He pretended so successfully to be virtuous.'
31. *his conversation . . . wife!* His adultery with Mistress Shore, citizen's wife, might be expected to make the citizens disapprove him.
32. *from:* free from.
attainder: stain that would dishonour him.
suspects: suspicions.
33. *Well, well:* Buckingham is pretending to be impatient with Richar moralising. Their 'double act' is meant to present Richard to mayor as utterly virtuous, even naïve.
covert'st shelter'd: most successfully camouflaged, and theref extremely cunning.
35. *almost:* even.

Gloucester
Look to the drawbridge there!
Buckingham
Hark! a drum.
Gloucester
Catesby, o'erlook the walls.
Buckingham
Lord Mayor, the reason we have sent—
Gloucester
Look back, defend thee; here are enemies.
Buckingham
God and our innocence defend and guard us!

Enter LOVEL *and* RATCLIFF, *with* HASTINGS' *head*

Gloucester
Be patient; they are friends—Ratcliff and Lovel.
Lovel
Here is the head of that ignoble traitor,
The dangerous and unsuspected Hastings.
Gloucester
So dear I lov'd the man that I must weep.
I took him for the plainest harmless creature
That breath'd upon the earth a Christian;
Made him my book, wherein my soul recorded
The history of all her secret thoughts.
So smooth he daub'd his vice with show of virtue
That, his apparent open guilt omitted,
I mean his conversation with Shore's wife—
He liv'd from all attainder of suspects.
Buckingham
Well, well, he was the covert'st shelter'd traitor
That ever liv'd.
Would you imagine, or almost believe—
Were't not that by great preservation
We live to tell it—that the subtle traitor
This day had plotted, in the council-house,
To murder me and my good Lord of Gloucester.

40. 'Had he plotted to do this?'

41. *Turks and Infidels:* Turks and any other people who were not Christian would be expected to behave brutally, without Christian love and humanity.
42. *against . . . law:* without going through the proper legal procedures.
43. *rashly:* hastily, hurriedly.

50. Richard's guess that the adultery with Mistress Shore would be an important consideration seems to have been correct.

52-61. Now that the mayor, sincerely or not, has accepted their accusation against Hastings, Buckingham and Richard can make their position more secure by raising the doubts the mayor himself ought to have raised, and obliging him to accept their excuses—without any proof at all, Buckingham also instructs the mayor in what he must do to help Richard.
52. 'But we had decided that he should not die . . .'
54. *our friends:* Ratcliff and Lovel, who are now taking the blame.
55. *Something . . . meanings:* rather misunderstanding what we intended.
57. *timorously:* with fear and trembling.
59. *signified:* reported.
60. *haply:* perhaps, quite likely.
61. *Misconster . . . him:* misunderstand our intentions when they see what we have done to him.
62-6. Does the mayor, do you think, really believe them? See Act III, Scene vi and Scene vii. What sort of man is he? Does he really represent the citizens' opinions?

66. *cause:* a legal case.
68. *carping:* always ready to find fault.
69-71. These lines sum up well the arrogant attitude of Richard and Buckingham to the rest. They do not care whether they are believed or not, as long as they appear to be believed. There is a complete lack of real concern, so that they can dismiss the mayor quite brusquely and impudently.
69. 'But since you come later than we intended for this purpose.'

Mayor

Had he done so?

Gloucester

What! think you we are Turks or Infidels?
Or that we would, against the form of law,
Proceed thus rashly in the villain's death
But that the extreme peril of the case,
The peace of England and our persons' safety,
Enforc'd us to this execution?

Mayor

Now, fair befall you! He deserv'd his death;
And your good Graces both have well proceeded
To warn false traitors from the like attempts.
I never look'd for better at his hands
After he once fell in with Mistress Shore.

Buckingham

Yet had we not determin'd he should die
Until your lordship came to see his end—
Which now the loving haste of these our friends,
Something against our meanings, have prevented—
Because, my lord, I would have had you heard
The traitor speak, and timorously confess
The manner and the purpose of his treasons:
That you might well have signified the same
Unto the citizens, who haply may
Misconster us in him and wail his death.

Mayor

But, my good lord, your Grace's words shall serve
As well as I had seen and heard him speak;
And do not doubt, right noble Princes both,
But I'll acquaint our duteous citizens
With all your just proceedings in this cause.

Gloucester

And to that end we wish'd your lordship here,
T' avoid the censures of the carping world.

Buckingham

Which since you come too late of our intent,

73. *hies him in all post:* goes quickly.

74. *at your . . . time:* making the most of the chances you get.

75. *infer:* suggest, speak of.

76-9. The citizen was a shopkeeper and the sign over his shop was crown. He meant that his son would inherit his business.

80. *urge:* emphasize, say a lot about.
luxury: lust.
81. 'His promiscuity, which was like an animal's'.
82. *their:* the citizens'.
83. *raging:* mad with lust.
savage: uncontrolled, not like a civilized man's.

85. *for a need:* if it is necessary.
come . . . person: refer to things that might affect my reputation (sin I am his brother).
86. *went with child:* was pregnant.
87. *insatiate:* never satisfied sexually.

89. *computation:* calculation.

90. *the issue . . . begot:* the child was not fathered by him.

91. *lineaments:* features, appearance.

94. Richard probably knows that his mother could refute the story, he doesn't want too much made of it.

96. *the golden fee:* the crown.

98. *Baynard's Castle* had been the London house of Richard, Duke York, father of Richard, Duke of Gloucester.
100. Richard is now all set for his next bit of acting. After being t watchful defender of the realm, he is to play the part of the devot religious man.
reverend fathers: priests.

Yet witness what you hear we did intend.
And so, my good Lord Mayor, we bid farewell.

Exit LORD MAYOR

Gloucester

Go, after, after, cousin Buckingham.
The Mayor towards Guildhall hies him in all post.
There, at your meet'st advantage of the time,
Infer the bastardy of Edward's children.
Tell them how Edward put to death a citizen
Only for saying he would make his son
Heir to the crown—meaning indeed his house,
Which by the sign thereof was termed so.
Moreover, urge his hateful luxury
And bestial appetite in change of lust,
Which stretch'd unto their servants, daughters, wives,
Even where his raging eye or savage heart
Without control lusted to make a prey.
Nay, for a need, thus far come near my person:
Tell them, when that my mother went with child
Of that insatiate Edward, noble York
My princely father then had wars in France
And, by true computation of the time,
Found that the issue was not his begot;
Which well appeared in his lineaments,
Being nothing like the noble Duke my father.
Yet touch this sparingly, as 'twere far off;
Because, my lord, you know my mother lives.

Buckingham

Doubt not, my lord, I'll play the orator
As if the golden fee for which I plead
Were for myself; and so, my lord, adieu.

Gloucester

If you thrive well, bring them to Baynard's Castle;
Where you shall find me well accompanied
With reverend fathers and well learned bishops.

102. *Guildhall:* the meeting place of the council that ruled the city.

103-4. *Dr Shaw* and *Friar Penker* were two of the priests who were going to accompany him so that he would appear to be pious.

106. *privy:* secret.
107. *brats:* a scornful word for children.
108. *no manner person:* no man, whatever his rank.
109. *recourse unto:* access to, opportunity of speaking to.
the Princes: Edward, Prince of Wales, and the Duke of York, who are in the Tower. They and Clarence's children, being the children of Richard's elder brothers, all had a better claim to the throne than he had.

SCENE VI

This short scene has two purposes: it reminds us of the illegality of the actions against Hastings; and it shows us that the ordinary citizen is not deceived by the cleverness of Richard, but is powerless to act against him.
Stage Direction. A *scrivener* was a professional writer and copier of documents.
1. *indictment:* the list of crimes he is charged with.
2. *set hand:* a style of handwriting used for official documents.
fairly is engrossed: written out in full in a formal way (a 'fair copy').
3. Official notices were often read in or near St Paul's cathedral.
4. *sequel:* sequence of events.
7. *the precedent:* the first version.
was . . . a-doing: took quite as long to do.
9. *Untainted:* unaccused.

10. *Here's . . . while!* What a good world we live in these days!
gross: stupid.
11. *palpable device:* obvious trick.

14. *in thought:* in silence.

Buckingham
I go; and towards three or four o'clock
Look for the news that the Guildhall affords.

Exit

Gloucester
Go, Lovel, with all speed to Doctor Shaw.
[*To* CATESBY] Go thou to Friar Penker. Bid them both
Meet me within this hour at Baynard's Castle.

Exeunt all but GLOUCESTER

Now will I go to take some privy order
To draw the brats of Clarence out of sight,
And to give order that no manner person
Have any time recourse unto the Princes.

Exit

CENE VI—*London. A street*

Enter a SCRIVENER

crivener
Here is the indictment of the good Lord Hastings;
Which in a set hand fairly is engross'd
That it may be to-day read o'er in Paul's.
And mark how well the sequel hangs together:
Eleven hours I have spent to write it over,
For yesternight by Catesby was it sent me;
The precedent was full as long a-doing;
And yet within these five hours Hastings liv'd,
Untainted, unexamin'd, free, at liberty.
Here's a good world the while! Who is so gross
That cannot see this palpable device?
Yet who's so bold but says he sees it not?
Bad is the world; and all will come to nought,
When such ill dealing must be seen in thought.

Exit

SCENE VII

There are three kinds of satisfaction that Richard gets from this episode: the humour of playing a holy man; the working for his own ambitions; and the manipulation of others. This is the last time that we see Richard enjoying the humour of a situation, and it is the point from which he begins to decline. The citizens are not, in fact, won over (lines 24-6) though he does manage to get what he wants (lines 239-240). He is at last beginning to fail, although he is far from being beaten.

3. Richard has met opponents who will not easily do what he wishes.
4. *Touch'd you . . .:* did you refer to . . .
5. Edward IV had, according to the Duchess of York, been engaged to marry Dame Elizabeth Lucy who had a child by him. He could not, according to the church's law, then marry Lady Elizabeth Grey. Their children were, therefore, bastards.

6. *in France:* i.e. with the Lady Bona, referred to again in line 181.

8. *enforcement:* rape.

9. *His tyranny . . . trifles:* his use of his power to get his own way even in little things.

12. *withal:* at the same time.
infer: refer to.
lineaments: characteristics.
14. *form:* build, physique.
15. Richard had been a very skilful and successful general in campaign against the Scots. Scotland was an independent kingdom at this time
16. *wisdom in peace:* Richard was the ruler of the northern counties o England on his brother's behalf.
17. *humility:* humanity. Richard, as his brother's deputy, did, in history show the qualities that Buckingham mentions.
18-19. 'I put forward every possible argument in your favour.'

22. If they had done this, Richard would have been able to claim that h had popular support for taking the crown.

SCENE VII—*London. Baynard's Castle*

Enter GLOUCESTER *and* BUCKINGHAM, *at several doors*

Gloucester
How now, how now! What say the citizens?
Buckingham
Now, by the holy Mother of our Lord,
The citizens are mum, say not a word.
Gloucester
Touch'd you the bastardy of Edward's children?
Buckingham
I did; with his contract with Lady Lucy,
And his contract by deputy in France;
Th' insatiate greediness of his desire,
And his enforcement of the city wives;
His tyranny for trifles; his own bastardy,
As being got, your father then in France,
And his resemblance, being not like the Duke.
Withal I did infer your lineaments,
Being the right idea of your father,
Both in your form and nobleness of mind;
Laid upon all your victories in Scotland,
Your discipline in war, wisdom in peace,
Your bounty, virtue, fair humility;
Indeed, left nothing fitting for your purpose
Untouch'd or slightly handled in discourse.
And when mine oratory drew toward end
I bid them that did love their country's good
Cry 'God save Richard, England's royal King!'
Gloucester
And did they so?
Buckingham
No, so God help me, they spake not a word;
But, like dumb statues or breathing stones,

26. *and look'd . . . pale:* Why? Were they afraid of what might happen if they did not do what Buckingham wanted? Or were they shocked by the dishonesty of the trick and the fact that they could do nothing about it? Or were they afraid of what was obviously going to happen?
27. *reprehended:* told off.
28. *wilful:* stubborn.
30. *Recorder:* a lawyer employed by the city council.

33. *in warrant . . . himself:* on his own responsibility, as though he agreed with it.
34. *followers:* servants, who had, of course, been placed there for this purpose.

37. *the vantage of:* the chance given by.

42. *tongueless blocks:* silent like lumps of rock or wood.

44. *at hand:* close by.
Intend some fear: Pretend that you feel unsafe.
44-50. Buckingham, probably unnecessarily, is offering Richard advice on how to play his part. These instructions tell how the episode is to be acted later.
45. *but by . . . suit:* except after very strong pleading.
48. *ground* and *descant* are both musical terms. The ground is the bass line of the tune above which the descant is sung. The descant is usually more decorative.
50. *maid:* virgin.

51-2. *if you . . . myself:* if you play your part as well as I play mine.

53. *issue:* result.

54. *leads:* a gallery, probably at first-floor level. The floor of the gallery would be the roof of the rooms or corridor below, and would be covered with lead to keep water out.
the Lord Mayor knocks: i.e. at an outer gate.

Stage Direction. *Aldermen* were leading citizens who took part in governing the city.

Star'd each on other, and look'd deadly pale.
Which when I saw, I reprehended them,
And ask'd the Mayor what meant this wilful silence.
His answer was, the people were not used
To be spoke to but by the Recorder.
Then he was urg'd to tell my tale again.
'Thus saith the Duke, thus hath the Duke inferr'd'—
But nothing spoke in warrant from himself.
When he had done, some followers of mine own
At lower end of the hall hurl'd up their caps,
And some ten voices cried 'God save King Richard!'
And thus I took the vantage of those few—
'Thanks, gentle citizens and friends', quoth I
'This general applause and cheerful shout
Argues your wisdoms and your love to Richard'.
And even here brake off and came away.

Gloucester

What, tongueless blocks were they? Would they not speak?
Will not the Mayor then and his brethren come?

Buckingham

The Mayor is here at hand. Intend some fear;
Be not you spoke with but by mighty suit;
And look you get a prayer-book in your hand,
And stand between two churchmen, good my lord;
For on that ground I'll make a holy descant;
And be not easily won to our requests.
Play the maid's part: still answer nay, and take it.

Gloucester

I go; and if you plead as well for them
As I can say nay to thee for myself,
No doubt we bring it to a happy issue.

Buckingham

Go, go, up to the leads; the Lord Mayor knocks.

Exit GLOUCESTER. *Enter the* LORD MAYOR, ALDERMEN, *and* CITIZENS

55. *I dance attendance:* I am waiting to get in.

56. *withal:* with.

61. *divinely . . . meditation:* like a holy man, devoting himself to religious thought.

62. *worldly suits:* affairs of the world.

66. *deep designs:* very serious concerns.
moment: importance.

67. *No less importing:* which concern nothing less.

69. *straight:* immediately.

71. 'He is not lying idly in bed making love immorally.'

73. 'Nor playing about with a couple of prostitutes.'

74. *deep:* learned.

75. *engross:* make fat.

76. *watchful:* wakeful, unsleeping.

78. *thereof:* i.e. of England.

80. *defend:* forbid.

Welcome, my lord. I dance attendance here;
I think the Duke will not be spoke withal.

Enter CATESBY

Now, Catesby, what says your lord to my request?

Catesby

He doth entreat your Grace, my noble lord,
To visit him to-morrow or next day.
He is within, with two right reverend fathers,
Divinely bent to meditation;
And in no worldly suits would he be mov'd,
To draw him from his holy exercise.

Buckingham

Return, good Catesby, to the gracious Duke;
Tell him, myself, the Mayor and Aldermen,
In deep designs, in matter of great moment,
No less importing than our general good,
Are come to have some conference with his Grace.

Catesby

I'll signify so much unto him straight.

Exit

Buckingham

Ah ha, my lord, this prince is not an Edward!
He is not lolling on a lewd love-bed,
But on his knees at meditation;
Not dallying with a brace of courtezans,
But meditating with two deep divines;
Not sleeping, to engross his idle body,
But praying, to enrich his watchful soul.
Happy were England would this virtuous prince
Take on his Grace the sovereignty thereof;
But, sure, I fear we shall not win him to it.

Lord Mayor

Marry, God defend his Grace should say us nay!

Buckingham

I fear he will. Here Catesby comes again.

Re-enter CATESBY

83. *to what end:* for what purpose.

92. *at their beads:* at prayer. Catholics carry a string of beads which they use to help them to concentrate on their prayers.
'tis much . . . thence: it is a difficult thing to drag them away.
93. *zealous:* devoted, keenly pious.

Stage Direction. There seems to be some doubt whether, when the play was first performed, the stage had a balcony. Normally, the balcony at the back of the stage would have been used for this kind of scene.

94. It is part of Buckingham's plan that the mayor, and not Buckingham himself, should draw the citizens' attention to Richard.

98. *ornaments:* He is referring to the prayer-book and the bishops.

99. *Plantagenet:* Richard's family name.

106. *deferr'd:* put off. He made his friends wait.

Now, Catesby, what says his Grace?

Catesby

My lord,
He wonders to what end you have assembled
Such troops of citizens to come to him.
His Grace not being warn'd thereof before,
He fears, my lord, you mean no good to him.

Buckingham

Sorry I am my noble cousin should
Suspect me that I mean no good to him.
By heaven, we come to him in perfect love;
And so once more return and tell his Grace.

Exit CATESBY

When holy and devout religious men
Are at their beads, 'tis much to draw them thence,
So sweet is zealous contemplation.

Enter GLOUCESTER *aloft, between two* BISHOPS

CATESBY *returns*

Lord Mayor

See where his Grace stands 'tween two clergymen!

Buckingham

Two props of virtue for a Christian prince,
To stay him from the fall of vanity;
And, see, a book of prayer in his hand,
True ornaments to know a holy man.
Famous Plantagenet, most gracious Prince,
Lend favourable ear to our requests,
And pardon us the interruption
Of thy devotion and right Christian zeal.

Gloucester

My lord, there needs no such apology:
I do beseech your Grace to pardon me,
Who, earnest in the service of my God,
Deferr'd the visitation of my friends.
But, leaving this, what is your Grace's pleasure?

109. *ungovern'd:* without a ruler. But it also suggests that it is becoming unruly.

110-12. Richard plays the part for all it is worth, pretending not only that he does not understand but also that he is guilty of some offence. The irony of the whole thing amuses him.
111. *disgracious:* displeasing.
112. *reprehend:* rebuke, tell off.

114. *amend:* put right.

115. 'For what other purpose do I live and claim to be a Christian?'

118. *sceptred:* The sceptre, a staff, is one of the insignia given to a king as a symbol of his power.
119. 'The good fortune that you deserve and ought to enjoy, and the position that is rightly yours by birth.'
120. *lineal glory:* the honour descending by inheritance.
121. *blemish'd stock:* Edward's allegedly bastard sons. A stock is a stem on which other plants are grafted. The word takes up again the image of growing trees, often found in the history plays. It continues in lines 124 and 126.
124-6. These three statements all refer to the supposed bastardy of Edward's children.
124. *want . . . limbs:* The branches of the tree are not its own; they are grafted on. See line 126.
125. *infamy:* shame.
127-8. Is it the throne, the country, or the family that is being forgotten? The confusion may occur as the result of Shakespeare's carelessness, or it may be that Buckingham has no intention of being clearer.
128. *oblivion:* unconsciousness.
129. *recure:* put right.
130. *charge:* responsibility for.

133. *lowly factor:* humble workman.
134. *successively:* by right of succession.

138. *by . . . instigation:* at their eager suggestion. We must not forget Buckingham's earlier report of their behaviour.

Buckingham

Even that, I hope, which pleaseth God above,
And all good men of this ungovern'd isle.

Gloucester

I do suspect I have done some offence
That seems disgracious in the city's eye,
And that you come to reprehend my ignorance.

Buckingham

You have, my lord. Would it might please your Grace,
On our entreaties, to amend your fault!

Gloucester

Else wherefore breathe I in a Christian land?

Buckingham

Know then, it is your fault that you resign
The supreme seat, the throne majestical,
The sceptred office of your ancestors,
Your state of fortune and your due of birth,
The lineal glory of your royal house,
To the corruption of a blemish'd stock;
Whiles in the mildness of your sleepy thoughts,
Which here we waken to our country's good,
The noble isle doth want her proper limbs;
Her face defac'd with scars of infamy,
Her royal stock graft with ignoble plants,
And almost shoulder'd in the swallowing gulf
Of dark forgetfulness and deep oblivion.
Which to recure, we heartily solicit
Your gracious self to take on you the charge
And kingly government of this your land—
Not as protector, steward, substitute,
Or lowly factor for another's gain;
But as successively, from blood to blood,
Your right of birth, your empery, your own.
For this, consorted with the citizens,
Your very worshipful and loving friends,
And by their vehement instigation,
In this just cause come I to move your Grace.

141. *in your reproof:* to criticize you.

142. *degree:* rank.

143. *haply:* perhaps.

144. *yielded:* Richard means yielded to their request.

146. *fondly:* foolishly and mistakenly.

148. *season'd:* spiced or flavoured, and, like food, thus made more attractive.

151. *not to . . . last:* i.e. not to speak ill of his friends.

152. *definitively:* this is my last word on the subject.

153-4. *my desert . . . request:* I do not deserve the honour, and so I turn down your request.

156. *even:* smooth.

157. *ripe revenue:* something he owns that is now ready for him to enjoy.

161. *bark:* ship.
brook: stand up to.

162-3. 'Than hope to have my faults hidden by the greatness of the office I held, and hidden from view by the splendour of it.' This is a glance at the favourite theme in Shakespeare of the relation of the man to his office.

165. *much . . . need:* I am short of many qualities that you would expect in me, if you needed help.

167. *stealing:* that pass without being noticed.

168. *become:* bring honour to.

170. *that:* that which.

172. *defend:* prevent.
wring: twist out of his hand.

174. 'The points you make are too subtle and unimportant.'

Gloucester

I cannot tell if to depart in silence
Or bitterly to speak in your reproof
Best fitteth my degree or your condition.
If not to answer, you might haply think
Tongue-tied ambition, not replying, yielded
To bear the golden yoke of sovereignty,
Which fondly you would here impose on me;
If to reprove you for this suit of yours,
So season'd with your faithful love to me,
Then, on the other side, I check'd my friends.
Therefore—to speak, and to avoid the first,
And then, in speaking, not to incur the last—
Definitively thus I answer you:
Your love deserves my thanks, but my desert
Unmeritable shuns your high request.
First, if all obstacles were cut away,
And that my path were even to the crown,
As the ripe revenue and due of birth,
Yet so much is my poverty of spirit,
So mighty and so many my defects,
That I would rather hide me from my greatness—
Being a bark to brook no mighty sea—
Than in my greatness covet to be hid,
And in the vapour of my glory smother'd.
But, God be thank'd, there is no need of me—
And much I need to help you, were there need.
The royal tree hath left us royal fruit
Which, mellow'd by the stealing hours of time,
Will well become the seat of majesty
And make, no doubt, us happy by his reign.
On him I lay that you would lay on me—
The right and fortune of his happy stars,
Which God defend that I should wring from him.

Buckingham

My lord, this argues conscience in your Grace;
But the respects thereof are nice and trivial,

183. *care-craz'd:* made mad with her worries.

184. *distressed:* poor.

186. *purchase:* reward.

187-8. 'Brought him down from the height of his great rank to a low position and a shameful, bigamous marriage.' The marriage was considered bigamous because he had already promised to marry someone else.

189. *got:* fathered.

191. *expostulate:* protest.

192. *save:* except.

to some alive: He means, of course, to Richard's mother. Remember that it was Richard's suggestion that Edward's illegitimacy should be mentioned (Act III, Scene v).

193. 'I restrain my tongue to spare others.'

195. 'This royal power which is offered t o you as yours by right.'

197-9. Buckingham means that if Richard takes the crown, a legitimate line will be restored, and his ancestors' shame be removed.

197. *draw forth:* rescue.

205. *take . . . amiss:* do not be offended.

All circumstances well considered.
You say that Edward is your brother's son.
So say we too, but not by Edward's wife;
For first was he contract to Lady Lucy—
Your mother lives a witness to his vow—
And afterward by substitute betroth'd
To Bona, sister to the King of France.
These both put off, a poor petitioner,
A care-craz'd mother to a many sons,
A beauty-waning and distressed widow,
Even in the afternoon of her best days,
Made prize and purchase of his wanton eye,
Seduc'd the pitch and height of his degree
To base declension and loath'd bigamy.
By her, in his unlawful bed, he got
This Edward, whom our manners call the Prince.
More bitterly could I expostulate,
Save that, for reverence to some alive,
I give a sparing limit to my tongue.
Then, good my lord, take to your royal self
This proffer'd benefit of dignity;
If not to bless us and the land withal,
Yet to draw forth your noble ancestry
From the corruption of abusing times
Unto a lineal true-derived course.

Lord Mayor
Do, good my lord; your citizens entreat you.

Buckingham
Refuse not, mighty lord, this proffer'd love.

Catesby
O, make them joyful, grant their lawful suit!

Gloucester
Alas, why would you heap this care on me?
I am unfit for state and majesty.
I do beseech you, take it not amiss:
I cannot nor I will not yield to you.

210. *effeminate remorse:* tender pity. It is effeminate because pity is thought of as a woman's emotion rather than a man's.

212. *egally:* equally.

213. *whe'er:* whether.

215-18. Buckingham's pretence of impatience would appear convincing to the mayor; particularly the rebellion against Richard and the threat to put someone else on the throne.

219. The hypocrisy of this, in its suggestion that Richard is shocked by mere swearing, and the fact that Richard can for so long stop himself from saying what he really wants to say, provide the comic climax to the scene.

221. *rue:* bitterly regret.

223. *Call them again:* The decision is in the end made in a hurry!

224. *penetrable to:* open to, i.e. he can be moved by pleading.

225. *albeit:* even though it is.

226. *sage:* wise.
grave: serious.

230-3. Richard is perhaps making a vain attempt to protect himself in advance from certain charges; but he must surely know that his crimes are so great that no-one would accept this excuse.
231. 'Come as the result of your putting this burden on me.'
232. 'The fact alone that you forced me will remove the guilt from me.'
234. *God doth know:* Obviously Richard uses this only as a form of words such as a holy man—as he pretends to be—might use; but it is important to the play that we believe that God *does* know, and will reward Richard accordingly.

Buckingham

If you refuse it—as, in love and zeal,
Loath to depose the child, your brother's son;
As well we know your tenderness of heart
And gentle, kind, effeminate remorse,
Which we have noted in you to your kindred
And egally indeed to all estates—
Yet know, whe'er you accept our suit or no,
Your brother's son shall never reign our king;
But we will plant some other in the throne
To the disgrace and downfall of your house;
And in this resolution here we leave you.
Come, citizens. Zounds, I'll entreat no more.

Gloucester

O, do not swear, my lord of Buckingham.

Exeunt BUCKINGHAM, MAYOR *and* CITIZENS

Catesby

Call him again, sweet Prince, accept their suit.
If you deny them, all the land will rue it.

Gloucester

Will you enforce me to a world of cares?
Call them again. I am not made of stones,
But penetrable to your kind entreaties,
Albeit against my conscience and my soul.

Re-enter BUCKINGHAM *and the* REST

Cousin of Buckingham, and sage grave men,
Since you will buckle fortune on my back,
To bear her burden, whe'er I will or no,
I must have patience to endure the load;
But if black scandal or foul-fac'd reproach
Attend the sequel of your imposition,
Your mere enforcement shall acquittance me
From all the impure blots and stains thereof;
For God doth know, and you may partly see,
How far I am from the desire of this.

Lord Mayor
God bless your Grace! We see it, and will say it.
Gloucester
In saying so, you shall but say the truth.
Buckingham
Then I salute you with this royal title—
Long live King Richard, England's worthy King!
All
Amen.
Buckingham
To-morrow may it please you to be crown'd?
Gloucester
Even when you please, for you will have it so.
Buckingham
To-morrow, then, we will attend your Grace;
And so, most joyfully, we take our leave.
Gloucester [*To the* BISHOPS]
Come, let us to our holy work again.
Farewell, my cousin; farewell, gentle friends.

Exeunt

ACT FOUR

SCENE I

The important thing to notice about this scene is that some of the women of the play—mothers, wives and daughters, all related to Richard in different ways—who would at another time be quarrelling with one another, begin to come together and share their hatred of Richard. Just at the time when he should be enjoying his greatest triumph, events and emotions begin to move effectively against him. The action of this scene prepares us for his greatest outrage, the murder of the young princes, and for the appearance of his successor, Henry, Earl of Richmond.

1. *niece Plantagenet:* Lady Margaret, Clarence's daughter, is in fact the Duchess's grand-daughter.

5. *Daughter:* Anne is, of course, Richard's wife.

10. *gratulate:* greet.

15. *By your patience:* If you will allow me to say so.

ACT FOUR

SCENE I—*London. Before the Tower*

Enter QUEEN ELIZABETH, DUCHESS OF YORK *and* MARQUIS OF DORSET, *at one door;* ANNE DUCHESS OF GLOUCESTER, *leading* LADY MARGARET PLANTAGENET, CLARENCE'S *young daughter, at another door*

Duchess of York
Who meets us here? My niece Plantagenet,
Led in the hand of her kind aunt of Gloucester?
Now, for my life, she's wand'ring to the Tower,
On pure heart's love, to greet the tender Princes.
Daughter, well met.

Anne God give your Graces both
A happy and a joyful time of day!

Queen Elizabeth
As much to you, good sister! Whither away?

Anne
No farther than the Tower; and, as I guess,
Upon the like devotion as yourselves,
To gratulate the gentle Princes there.

Queen Elizabeth
Kind sister, thanks, we'll enter all together.

Enter BRAKENBURY

And in good time, here the lieutenant comes.
Master Lieutenant, pray you, by your leave,
How doth the Prince, and my young son of York?

Brakenbury
Right well, dear madam. By your patience,
I may not suffer you to visit them.
The King hath strictly charg'd the contrary.

18. The people in the most useful positions already know what is happening; those who, we might think, ought to know, do not yet know of Richard's intended accession.

20. *bounds:* barriers.

24. *thy blame:* the blame that may fall on you.

25. 'I will run the risk of taking on your job (of guarding them).'

26. *it:* the office, duties.

30. *reverend:* worthy of respect.
looker-on: watcher.

33. The bodice of her dress would be pulled tight by laces.

34. *pent:* confined.

36. *Despiteful:* cruel. We would say, spiteful.

37. *Be . . . cheer:* If we take Dorset's suggestion to 'Look on the bright side of things' as addressed to Anne, it is not such a silly remark, since she will have the honour and dignity of queen.

39. *dogs:* follows closely. The image is of a hunting dog keeping close behind what he is hunting.

40. *is ominous:* brings bad luck.

Queen Elizabeth
The King! Who's that?
Brakenbury I mean the Lord Protector.
Queen Elizabeth
The Lord protect him from that kingly title!
Hath he set bounds between their love and me?
I am their mother; who shall bar me from them?
Duchess of York
I am their father's mother; I will see them.
Anne
Their aunt I am in law, in love their mother.
Then bring me to their sights; I'll bear thy blame,
And take thy office from thee on my peril.
Brakenbury
No, madam, no. I may not leave it so;
I am bound by oath, and therefore pardon me.

Exit. Enter STANLEY

Stanley
Let me but meet you, ladies, one hour hence,
And I'll salute your Grace of York as mother
And reverend looker-on of two fair queens.
[*To* ANNE] Come, madam, you must straight to Westminster,
There to be crowned Richard's royal queen.
Queen Elizabeth
Ah, cut my lace asunder
That my pent heart may have some scope to beat,
Or else I swoon with this dead-killing news!
Anne
Despiteful tidings! O unpleasing news!
Dorset
Be of good cheer; mother, how fares your Grace?
Queen Elizabeth
O Dorset, speak not to me, get thee gone!
Death and destruction dogs thee at thy heels;
Thy mother's name is ominous to children.

41. *outstrip:* run faster than. This continues the idea begun with 'dogs' in line 39.
42. *Richmond:* Henry, Earl of Richmond, who, after the battle at Tewkesbury had been sent to Brittany. He now begins to appear as a possible opponent of Richard.
43. *hie thee:* go away from here in a hurry.
44. *increase:* She means by being killed herself.
45. *thrall:* someone under the complete control of another. This is the third reference to the fulfilment of the curse in Act I, Scene iii. It is echoed in line 46.
46. *counted:* accepted.
47. *care:* concern.

49. *You:* Dorset.
my son: Richmond. Stanley was married to the Countess of Richmond, whose previous husband was Henry's father.
51. *ta'en tardy:* taken by surprise.

52. *ill-dispersing:* scattering in this evil way.

53. *bed of death:* birth-place of death.

54. *cockatrice:* the same as a basilisk, a mythical reptile that could kill with a look.

58. *inclusive verge:* rim that encloses something.

59. *round:* encircle.

60. *sear:* burn. An ancient method of punishing someone who killed a king was to put a crown of red-hot iron on his head.
61. *Anointed:* Part of the coronation ceremony was the anointing, the pouring of holy oil on the king's head.
venom: poison.

64. *humour:* feelings (of spite, here).

67. *his:* Richard's.

69. *dear saint:* Henry VI.

If thou wilt outstrip death, go cross the seas,
And live with Richmond, from the reach of hell.
Go, hie thee, hie thee from this slaughter-house,
Lest thou increase the number of the dead,
And make me die the thrall of Margaret's curse,
Nor mother, wife, nor England's counted queen.

Stanley

Full of wise care is this your counsel, madam.
Take all the swift advantage of the hours;
You shall have letters from me to my son
In your behalf, to meet you on the way.
Be not ta'en tardy by unwise delay.

Duchess of York

O ill-dispersing wind of misery!
O my accursed womb, the bed of death!
A cockatrice hast thou hatch'd to the world,
Whose unavoided eye is murderous.

Stanley

Come, madam, come; I in all haste was sent.

Anne

And I with all unwillingness will go.
O, would to God that the inclusive verge
Of golden metal that must round my brow
Were red-hot steel, to sear me to the brains!
Anointed let me be with deadly venom,
And die ere men can say 'God save the Queen!'

Queen Elizabeth

Go, go, poor soul; I envy not thy glory.
To feed my humour, wish thyself no harm.

Anne

No, why? When he that is my husband now
Came to me, as I follow'd Henry's corse;
When scarce the blood was well wash'd from his hands
Which issued from my other angel husband,
And that dear saint which then I weeping follow'd—
O, when, I say, I look'd on Richard's face,
This was my wish: 'Be thou' quoth I 'accurs'd

72. *so old a widow:* Because time had passed so slowly since his death, she felt that she had been a widow many years; or his death so upset her, she had aged suddenly.

79. *Grossly:* behaving without any fine feelings. What does this tell us about Richard?

81. *hitherto:* right up to this moment.

84. *timorous:* full of fear. We see in Act V, Scene iii, before the battle, how Richard is disturbed by dreams.

87. *complaining:* sorrowful story.

89. Dorset is speaking to Anne.

90. Anne is speaking to Elizabeth.

95. *Eighty odd years:* a few more than eighty. This would have been a very great age for the time. Actually, she was sixty-eight at this time but lived until she was eighty.
96. 'For every hour of joy that I have had there has been a week o grief.'
98. *tender babes:* As any mother does, Queen Elizabeth, in the time o their trouble, thinks of her children as being particularly young an helpless.
99. *envy:* hatred.
immur'd: imprisoned.

For making me, so young, so old a widow;
And when thou wed'st, let sorrow haunt thy bed;
And be thy wife, if any be so mad,
More miserable by the life of thee
Than thou hast made me by my dear lord's death'.
Lo, ere I can repeat this curse again,
Within so small a time, my woman's heart
Grossly grew captive to his honey words
And prov'd the subject of mine own soul's curse,
Which hitherto hath held my eyes from rest;
For never yet one hour in his bed
Did I enjoy the golden dew of sleep,
But with his timorous dreams was still awak'd.
Besides, he hates me for my father Warwick;
And will, no doubt, shortly be rid of me.

Queen Elizabeth
Poor heart, adieu! I pity thy complaining.

Anne
No more than with my soul I mourn for yours.

Dorset
Farewell, thou woeful welcomer of glory!

Anne
Adieu, poor soul, that tak'st thy leave of it!

Duchess of York [*To* DORSET]
Go thou to Richmond, and good fortune guide thee!
[*To* ANNE] Go thou to Richard, and good angels tend thee!
[*To* QUEEN ELIZABETH] Go thou to sanctuary, and good thoughts possess thee!
I to my grave, where peace and rest lie with me!
Eighty odd years of sorrow have I seen,
And each hour's joy wreck'd with a week of teen.

Queen Elizabeth
Stay, yet look back with me unto the Tower.
Pity, you ancient stones, those tender babes
Whom envy hath immur'd within your walls,
Rough cradle for such little pretty ones.

101. *Rude:* rough.
ragged: rugged, rough.
sullen: unsmiling. She is still speaking about the Tower itself.

SCENE II

Richard in making his way to the throne has punished others for their past sins: now, he has to be punished for his own. After the banding together of the women in the last scene, we now see Buckingham refusing to do as he is asked. Unlike Hastings he is not punished immediately by Richard, but is allowed to escape. This, we might think, shows Richard—despite all the other things he does—beginning to lose control.

Stage Direction. *Richard in pomp:* Richard is dressed in crown and coronation robes.

1. *Stand all apart:* everyone stand back.

Stage Direction. The throne would be on a dais, possibly up several steps.

5. Richard is, of course, very conscious that kings can be deposed and even murdered. The princes in the Tower are an obvious rallying point for those who hate him.

7. *Still live they:* May they continue to live!

8. *play the touch:* act as a touchstone, a piece of rock (usually dark quartz) on which metals could be tested. Gold and silver alloys were scraped on to such a stone and the streak of metal examined.
9. *current:* accepted as genuine.
10. Richard does not usually hesitate to say quite clearly what his evil intentions are. Does this reluctance here mean that even he has some shame about the murdering of the princes; or is he just testing Buckingham?
12. *I would be King:* I wish really to be king.

Rude ragged nurse, old sullen playfellow
For tender princes, use my babies well.
So foolish sorrows bids your stones farewell.

Exeunt

SCENE II—*London. The palace*

Sound a sennet. Enter RICHARD, *in pomp, as King;* BUCKINGHAM, CATESBY, RATCLIFF, LOVEL, *a* PAGE *and* OTHERS

King Richard
Stand all apart. Cousin of Buckingham!

Buckingham
My gracious sovereign?

King Richard
Give me thy hand. [*Here he ascendeth the throne. Sound*]
Thus high, by thy advice
And thy assistance, is King Richard seated.
But shall we wear these glories for a day;
Or shall they last, and we rejoice in them?

Buckingham
Still live they, and for ever let them last!

King Richard
Ah, Buckingham, now do I play the touch,
To try if thou be current gold indeed.
Young Edward lives—think now what I would speak.

Buckingham
Say on, my loving lord.

King Richard
Why, Buckingham, I say I would be King.

Buckingham
Why, so you are, my thrice-renowned lord.

King Richard
Ha! am I King? 'Tis so; but Edward lives.

15. Buckingham must know what Richard means, yet he cannot find an answer that will stop Richard from becoming angrier. His flattering titles for Richard—though Buckingham has always been inclined to use them—are something for him to say without having to answer 'yes' or 'no'.
consequence: sequence of ideas.
16. *true noble Prince:* Richard's repetition of Buckingham's answer sneers at Buckingham (who must by now be feeling very unsure of himself); and also mocks Richard, by reminding him who the rightful heir is.
17. 'In the past you were not so slow to understand.'
18. *the bastards:* Since Richard is speaking privately to Buckingham, his calling the princes 'bastards' suggests that he is trying to convince himself that his act is perhaps justifiable.
19. *suddenly:* quickly, promptly.
22-3. Richard is menacingly sarcastic.

25. *positively speak:* speak in agreement.

26. *resolve you:* give you my decision.
presently: immediately.

28. *iron-witted:* stupid.

29. *unrespective:* thoughtless.
29-30. *none . . . eyes:* I will have nothing to do with those who examine me closely with calculating looks.
31. *High-reaching:* ambitious.
circumspect: cautious.

35. *close:* secret.
exploit: action that calls for courage.

37. *haughty:* proud.

Buckingham
True, noble Prince.
King Richard O bitter consequence:
That Edward still should live—true noble Prince!
Cousin, thou wast not wont to be so dull.
Shall I be plain? I wish the bastards dead.
And I would have it suddenly perform'd.
What say'st thou now? Speak suddenly, be brief.
Buckingham
Your Grace may do your pleasure.
King Richard
Tut, tut, thou art all ice; thy kindness freezes.
Say, have I thy consent that they shall die?
Buckingham
Give me some little breath, some pause, dear lord,
Before I positively speak in this.
I will resolve you herein presently.

Exit

Catesby [*Aside to another*]
The King is angry; see, he gnaws his lip.
King Richard
I will converse with iron-witted fools

Descends from the throne

And unrespective boys; none are for me
That look into me with considerate eyes.
High-reaching Buckingham grows circumspect.
Boy!
Page
My lord?
King Richard
Know'st thou not any whom corrupting gold
Will tempt unto a close exploit of death?
Page
I know a discontented gentleman
Whose humble means match not his haughty spirit.

41. *partly:* slightly.

42. *deep-revolving:* cunning and calculating.
witty: clever.

44. *held out:* run beside me. A metaphor from hunting again.

47-9. Stanley, as we know, is less than frank here. This is the beginning of his tricking of Richard.

50-60. The speed with which Richard acts on this news is typical of that quickness of decision that makes him successful so often. It also suggests that he succeeds through careful planning.
52. *close:* shut up.

53. *mean:* of low social standing.

54. *straight:* immediately.

55. *The boy:* Clarence's son.
foolish: We would say, an idiot, using the word in its strict sense of a person who is mentally subnormal.
56. Catesby appears to be surprised, even shocked, by these orders, for he has to be told to pay attention again.
58. *it . . . upon:* it is very important to me.

60. *my brother's:* Edward IV's.

Gold were as good as twenty orators,
And will, no doubt, tempt him to anything.

King Richard
What is his name?

Page His name, my lord, is Tyrrel.

King Richard
I partly know the man. Go, call him hither, boy.

Exit PAGE

The deep-revolving witty Buckingham
No more shall be the neighbour to my counsels.
Hath he so long held out with me, untir'd,
And stops he now for breath? Well, be it so.

Enter STANLEY

How now, Lord Stanley! What's the news?

Stanley
Know, my loving lord,
The Marquis Dorset, as I hear, is fled
To Richmond, in the parts where he abides.

Stands apart

King Richard
Come hither, Catesby. Rumour it abroad
That Anne, my wife, is very grievous sick;
I will take order for her keeping close.
Inquire me out some mean poor gentleman,
Whom I will marry straight to Clarence' daughter—
The boy is foolish, and I fear not him.
Look how thou dream'st! I say again, give out
That Anne, my queen, is sick and like to die.
About it; for it stands me much upon
To stop all hopes whose growth may damage me.

Exit CATESBY

I must be married to my brother's daughter,
Or else my kingdom stands on brittle glass.

62. Even Richard finds this a strange way to behave.

63-4. *But . . . sin:* For the first time Richard is beginning to sound a little desperate.

68. Tyrrel's greeting is a formal, respectful greeting, but by using the words in their fullest sense Richard immediately gets down to business.

70. *Please you:* If you wish.

71. Tyrrel seems to know what he is being asked. He is even—does this show a loss of authority in Richard?—forcing Richard to come to the point.

73. We should remember Anne's comment in Act IV, Scene i.

74. *deal upon:* deal with.

76-7. Tyrrel remains unshocked. His lack of sentiment commends him to Richard; but it will also, when we remember it later, increase the horror of his act.

79. *this token:* Richard gives Tyrrel something that will prove that he comes from the king.
Rise: Tyrrel has been kneeling since he entered.

80. *no more but so:* nothing but that.

81. *prefer:* reward with promotion.

Murder her brothers, and then marry her!
Uncertain way of gain! But I am in
So far in blood that sin will pluck on sin.
Tear-falling pity dwells not in this eye.

Re-enter PAGE, *with* TYRREL

Is thy name Tyrrel?

Tyrrel

James Tyrrel, and your most obedient subject.

King Richard

Art thou, indeed?

Tyrrel Prove me, my gracious lord.

King Richard

Dar'st thou resolve to kill a friend of mine?

Tyrrel

Please you;
But I had rather kill two enemies.

King Richard

Why, then thou hast it. Two deep enemies,
Foes to my rest, and my sweet sleep's disturbers,
Are they that I would have thee deal upon.
Tyrrel, I mean those bastards in the Tower.

Tyrrel

Let me have open means to come to them,
And soon I'll rid you from the fear of them.

King Richard

Thou sing'st sweet music. Hark, come hither, Tyrrel.
Go, by this token. Rise, and lend thine ear.

Whispers

There is no more but so: say it is done,
And I will love thee and prefer thee for it.

Tyrrel

I will dispatch it straight.

Exit. Re-enter BUCKINGHAM

85. *Well . . . rest:* Another example of Richard's decisiveness. All Buckingham's past help is as good as forgotten.

87. *look unto it:* take care; do something about it. He is warning Stanley not to become involved in any revolt.

89. 'For which you have sworn on your honour and by your faith.'

93. *you . . . it:* you will be held responsible.

97. *peevish:* silly.

101. *him:* the prophet, who was King Henry VI.

106. *bard:* poet.

Buckingham

My lord, I have consider'd in my mind
The late request that you did sound me in.

King Richard

Well, let that rest. Dorset is fled to Richmond.

Buckingham

I hear the news, my lord.

King Richard

Stanley, he is your wife's son: well, look unto it.

Buckingham

My lord, I claim the gift, my due by promise,
For which your honour and your faith is pawn'd:
Th' earldom of Hereford and the movables
Which you have promised I shall possess.

King Richard

Stanley, look to your wife; if she convey
Letters to Richmond, you shall answer it.

Buckingham

What says your Highness to my just request?

King Richard

I do remember me: Henry the Sixth
Did prophesy that Richmond should be King,
When Richmond was a little peevish boy.
A king!—perhaps—

Buckingham

My lord—

King Richard

How chance the prophet could not at that time
Have told me, I being by, that I should kill him?

Buckingham

My lord, your promise for the earldom—

King Richard

Richmond! When last I was at Exeter,
The mayor in courtesy show'd me the castle
And call'd it Rugemount, at which name I started,
Because a bard of Ireland told me once
I should not live long after I saw Richmond.

109-16. Richard is being deliberately and coldly rude to Buckingham.

114-15. *thou . . . meditation:* 'you regularly, like a clock, interrupt my thoughts with your begging.'
114. *Jack:* There are two meanings here: (1) the figure of a man on a clock, that strikes the hours; (2) a low, common person.
116. *vein:* mood.

117. 'Would you please give an answer to my request?'

119. *deep:* that puts Richard under a great obligation.
120. *Made . . . this?* Buckingham, of course, exaggerates his own importance in the business. Buckingham has been a most useful ally, but without him Richard would have found some other way of getting what he wanted.
122. *Brecknock:* a manor in South Wales.

SCENE III

This scene is a mechanical functional one. In order to turn the plot in the right direction, much must be done and be reported to have been done, so that after the murder of the princes has been announced there is reference to Richard's wife's death, the fate of Clarence's children and the progress of Buckingham's rebellion.

Stage Direction. The scene follows immediately on the last one; there is no reference in the scene to any change of place.

1-22. Tyrrel's distress and remorse contrast with his callousness when he received his orders. They increase the audience's pity for the princes and the horror of Richard's crime.
2. *arch:* supreme.

Buckingham
My lord—
King Richard
Ay, what's o'clock?
Buckingham
I am thus bold to put your Grace in mind
Of what you promis'd me.
King Richard Well, but what's o'clock?
Buckingham
Upon the stroke of ten.
King Richard Well, let it strike.
Buckingham
Why let it strike?
King Richard
Because that like a Jack thou keep'st the stroke
Betwixt thy begging and my meditation.
I am not in the giving vein to-day.
Buckingham
May it please you to resolve me in my suit.
King Richard
Thou troublest me; I am not in the vein.

Exeunt all but BUCKINGHAM

Buckingham
And is it thus? Repays he my deep service
With such contempt? Made I him King for this?
O, let me think on Hastings, and be gone
To Brecknock while my fearful head is on!

Exit

SCENE III—*London. The palace*

Enter TYRREL

Tyrrel
The tyrannous and bloody act is done,
The most arch deed of piteous massacre

4. *suborn:* bribe.

5. *piece:* masterpiece.

6. *flesh'd:* experienced. Another image from hunting. The hunting birds and animals were given flesh to eat.

11. *alabaster:* a white or pink stone, with slightly darker lines, like veins.

13. *summer:* the season for roses.

18. *replenished:* filled with nature's beauties.

19. 'That Nature ever made since she first created the world.'

25-7. Although this may be no more than a proper and courteous way of answering the king, yet it can also be seen as Tyrrel coming as near as he dare to telling the king of his horror.

25. *gave in charge:* ordered me to do.

That ever yet this land was guilty of.
Dighton and Forrest, who I did suborn
To do this piece of ruthless butchery,
Albeit they were flesh'd villains, bloody dogs,
Melted with tenderness and mild compassion,
Wept like two children in their deaths' sad story.
'O, thus' quoth Dighton 'lay the gentle babes'—
'Thus, thus,' quoth Forrest 'girdling one another
Within their alabaster innocent arms.
Their lips were four red roses on a stalk,
And in their summer beauty kiss'd each other.
A book of prayers on their pillow lay;
Which once,' quoth Forrest 'almost chang'd my mind;
But, O, the devil'—there the villain stopp'd;
When Dighton thus told on: 'We smothered
The most replenished sweet work of nature
That from the prime creation e'er she framed'.
Hence both are gone with conscience and remorse
They could not speak; and so I left them both,
To bear this tidings to the bloody King.

Enter KING RICHARD

And here he comes. All health, my sovereign lord!

King Richard
Kind Tyrrel, am I happy in thy news?

Tyrrel
If to have done the thing you gave in charge
Beget your happiness, be happy then,
For it is done.

King Richard
But didst thou see them dead?

Tyrrel
I did, my lord.

King Richard And buried, gentle Tyrrel?

Tyrrel
The chaplain of the Tower hath buried them;
But where, to say the truth, I do not know.

31. *soon at:* just before.
after supper: late supper, or the time between supper and bedtime.

36-9. Richard has done all that he proposed to do in Act IV, Scene ii.

37. *meanly:* basely, i.e. to someone below her social status.

40. *Britaine:* Breton, i.e. from Brittany, in northern France. Richard calls Richmond this for he has been in exile there.

42. *knot:* marriage.
looks . . . crown: has ambition that he may become king.
43. *thriving:* for whom things are going well. Richard is still pleased with himself although the list of his crimes grows longer and there are some hitches in his planning.

46. *Morton:* Thomas Morton, Bishop of Ely. Throughout his career he was a crafty politician.
47. *back'd with:* supported by.
hardy: tough.
48. *Is in the fields:* is on the march, and looking for his enemy.
power: army.
50. *rash-levied:* hastily raised.
51-5. In these lines we see the courage that is one of the mainsprings of his actions and that remains to the end an admirable quality.
51-2. 'Frightened discussion only leads to delay, and delay causes helpless ruin.' *Leaden*, *dull*, and *snail-paced* emphasize the idea of slowness.
54-5. 'Let swift, exciting action carry me forward. Just as Mercury, with his winged heels, was the herald of Jove, so swift action can be the herald of the king.'
Jove: the greatest of the Roman gods.

King Richard
Come to me, Tyrrel, soon at after supper,
When thou shalt tell the process of their death.
Meantime, but think how I may do thee good
And be inheritor of thy desire.
Farewell till then.

Tyrrel I humbly take my leave.

Exit

King Richard
The son of Clarence have I pent up close;
His daughter meanly have I match'd in marriage;
The sons of Edward sleep in Abraham's bosom,
And Anne my wife hath bid this world good night.
Now, for I know the Britaine Richmond aims
At young Elizabeth, my brother's daughter,
And by that knot looks proudly on the crown,
To her go I, a jolly thriving wooer.

Enter RATCLIFF

Ratcliff
My lord!

King Richard
Good or bad news, that thou com'st in so bluntly?

Ratcliff
Bad news, my lord: Morton is fled to Richmond;
And Buckingham, back'd with the hardy Welshmen,
Is in the field, and still his power increaseth.

King Richard
Ely with Richmond troubles me more near
Than Buckingham and his rash-levied strength.
Come, I have learn'd that fearful commenting
Is leaden servitor to dull delay;
Delay leads impotent and snail-pac'd beggary.
Then fiery expedition be my wing,
Jove's Mercury, and herald for a king!

56. *My . . . shield:* There is no time for discussion; we must fight.

SCENE IV

This scene falls into three sections, two of them reminding us of very early scenes in the play.

In the first part, the old Queen Margaret returns, and as in the earlier scene, after listening while she remains hidden, reminds the other women, now united in their hatred of Richard, that the curses she spoke in Act I, Scene iii, are now nearly all fulfilled. In her complete lack of human sympathy and her apparent control over events, she seems a creature from another world. The sense of something extraordinary is emphasized by the formality of the verse: the repetition of rhythms and words, and the similarities of the names used, hypnotize us. The mournful chanting of the women is a commentary on all the disasters of this and earlier reigns, and also a condemnation of the evil in men and women that causes suffering.

The second part of the scene reminds us of Act I, Scene, ii when Richard wooed his wife, the Lady Anne. The difference this time is that he cannot speak directly to the woman he wants to marry, but has to address her through her mother, Queen Elizabeth. This is his most difficult task yet, and his first important failure—though he does not realize that he has failed. Why does he fail? Perhaps because the person he is speaking to is not directly concerned; but also because he is trying too hard. This second marriage he regards as politically essential, so that his success is more important than it was when he was wooing Anne. Then he was only concerned to show what a 'clever chap' he was.

The third part moves the plot on and quickly deals with many important events; but it also shows us Richard at last losing control, agitated, and harassed.

1-2. Margaret is referring to the prosperity of her enemies.
1. *mellow:* change as it grows old (part of yet another plant image).
3. *in these confines:* near the palace.
4. *waning:* decline.
5-7. 'I have seen the opening of the play (in which my enemies suffer) and I will now withdraw to France, hoping that the rest of the play will be as tragic for them as the beginning.'
5. *induction:* prologue, introduction to a play.
8. *Withdraw thee:* She hides out of sight of the others, but able—as in Act I, Scene iii—to hear what they say. She does not show herself until line 35.
10. *unblown:* not fully open.
12. *doom perpetual:* eternal death.
15. *right for right:* the carrying out of justice.
16. The bright hopefulness of the children's youth is compared with the morning, and the desolation of their death, usually associated with the old, to night.

Go, muster men. My counsel is my shield.
We must be brief when traitors brave the field.

Exeunt

SCENE IV—*London. Before the palace*

Enter old QUEEN MARGARET

Queen Margaret

So now prosperity begins to mellow
And drop into the rotten mouth of death.
Here in these confines slily have I lurk'd
To watch the waning of mine enemies.
A dire induction am I witness to,
And will to France, hoping the consequence
Will prove as bitter, black, and tragical.
Withdraw thee, wretched Margaret. Who comes here?

Retires. Enter QUEEN ELIZABETH *and the* DUCHESS OF YORK

Queen Elizabeth

Ah, my poor princes! ah, my tender babes!
My unblown flowers, new-appearing sweets!
If yet your gentle souls fly in the air
And be not fix'd in doom perpetual,
Hover about me with your airy wings
And hear your mother's lamentation.

Queen Margaret

Hover about her; say that right for right
Hath dimm'd your infant morn to aged night.

17. *craz'd:* cracked.

19. *Edward Plantagenet:* the young King Edward V, her grandson.

20. Margaret's son, the Prince of Wales killed at Tewkesbury, was also called Edward Plantagenet.
doth quit: pays for.

23. *entrails:* bowels, intestines.
the wolf: Richard.
24. *When . . . sleep:* At what other time did you sleep?

25. *holy Harry:* King Henry VI, her husband.

26-8. The Duchess of York is referring to herself, battered by experience and misery, in all these expressions.

28. *abstract:* summary.

29. *unrest:* restlessness. Her griefs disturb her always.

31. *thou:* the earth.

32. *melancholy seat:* a place for her to sit and grieve. (She is addressing the soil of England.)

35. *reverend:* deserving respect.

36. *benefit of seniory:* the priority of age.

37. *on the upper hand:* in the most honoured place.

39. *Tell o'er:* count.

40. *an Edward:* Edward, Prince of Wales.

Duchess of York
So many miseries have craz'd my voice
That my woe-wearied tongue is still and mute.
Edward Plantagenet, why art thou dead?
Queen Margaret
Plantagenet doth quit Plantagenet,
Edward for Edward pays a dying debt.
Queen Elizabeth
Wilt thou, O God, fly from such gentle lambs
And throw them in the entrails of the wolf?
When didst thou sleep when such a deed was done?
Queen Margaret
When holy Harry died, and my sweet son.
Duchess of York
Dead life, blind sight, poor mortal living ghost,
Woe's scene, world's shame, grave's due by life usurp'd,
Brief abstract and record of tedious days,
Rest thy unrest on England's lawful earth,

Sitting down

Unlawfully made drunk with innocent blood.
Queen Elizabeth
Ah, that thou wouldst as soon afford a grave
As thou canst yield a melancholy seat!
Then would I hide my bones, not rest them here.
Ah, who hath any cause to mourn but we?

Sitting down by her

Queen Margaret [*Coming forward*]
If ancient sorrow be most reverend,
Give mine the benefit of seniory,
And let my griefs frown on the upper hand.
If sorrow can admit society,

Sitting down with them

Tell o'er your woes again by viewing mine.
I had an Edward, till a Richard kill'd him;

41. *a husband:* King Henry VI.

42. *Thou:* Queen Elizabeth.
an Edward: King Edward V.
43. *Thou:* Queen Elizabeth.
a Richard: the Duke of York, killed in the Tower.

44. *Richard:* her husband, father of Edward IV, Clarence and others.

45. *Rutland:* her youngest son.
holp'st: helped.

46. *Thou:* the Duchess of York.

49. It was said that Richard was born with teeth: the idea adds to the monstrous impression built up about him.
50. *worry:* attack.
lap: drink as animals do.
52. *excellent:* excelling all others in his tyranny.
53. *galled:* smarting, stinging.

55. *true-disposing:* who arranges things justly.

56. *How do I:* This is a forceful way of saying, 'How I do.'
carnal cur: flesh-eating dog.
57. *issue:* children.
58. 'Makes her sit and weep with others at a funeral.'

62. *cloy me:* make myself feel sick.

65. *but boot:* only something to make up the required amount.

70. *untimely:* before their proper time.

71. 'The only reason that he himself is not yet sent to hell is that he is the devil's agent.' *intelligencer:* secret agent.
72. *to buy souls:* He had, for example, corrupted Anne and Buckingham.

I had a husband, till a Richard kill'd him:
Thou hadst an Edward, till a Richard kill'd him;
Thou hadst a Richard, till a Richard kill'd him.

Duchess of York

I had a Richard too, and thou didst kill him;
I had a Rutland too, thou holp'st to kill him.

Queen Margaret

Thou hadst a Clarence too, and Richard kill'd him.
From forth the kennel of thy womb hath crept
A hell-hound that doth hunt us all to death.
That dog, that had his teeth before his eyes
To worry lambs and lap their gentle blood,
That foul defacer of God's handiwork,
That excellent grand tyrant of the earth
That reigns in galled eyes of weeping souls,
Thy womb let loose to chase us to our graves.
O upright, just, and true-disposing God,
How do I thank thee that this carnal cur
Preys on the issue of his mother's body
And makes her pew-fellow with others' moan!

Duchess of York

O Harry's wife, triumph not in my woes!
God witness with me, I have wept for thine.

Queen Margaret

Bear with me; I am hungry for revenge,
And now I cloy me with beholding it.
Thy Edward he is dead, that kill'd my Edward;
The other Edward dead, to quit my Edward;
Young York he is but boot, because both they
Match'd not the high perfection of my loss.
Thy Clarence he is dead that stabb'd my Edward;
And the beholders of this frantic play,
Th' adulterate Hastings, Rivers, Vaughan, Grey,
Untimely smother'd in their dusky graves.
Richard yet lives, hell's black intelligencer;
Only reserv'd their factor to buy souls
And send them thither. But at hand, at hand,

82-3. These lines repeat what Margaret said in Act I, Scene iii, lines 244-5.
83-5. The words *shadow*, *painted*, *presentation*, *index* (meaning a prologue or preface), and *pageant* are all words that were used in the theatre. Their purpose here is to suggest that a queen's splendour and majesty are false, and that truth will break through at some time, as it has done now for Elizabeth, and as it did for Margaret long ago.
86. The rest of the speech fills out this idea of the uncertainty of fortune, a moral that, because of its obvious truth, was often repeated by Shakespeare and others.
88. *garish:* brightly coloured, and therefore easily seen and aimed at. *flag:* standard-bearer.
89. *shot:* someone who can shoot well.

94. *sues:* begs.

95. *bending peers:* nobles humbling themselves.

96. *thronging troops:* crowds.

97. *Decline all this:* read all this through from beginning to end.

98. *For:* instead of.

99. *wails the name:* is distressed at being called (a mother).

101. *caitiff:* wretched person.

103. *one:* Richard.

105. 'In this way the carrying out of justice has brought about changes.'

106-8 'As time passes things can only be worse for you, as you will be able to think only of what good fortune you had, and this will be all the more distressing to you when you realise what you are suffering at the time.'

Ensues his piteous and unpitied end.
Earth gapes, hell burns, fiends roar, saints pray,
To have him suddenly convey'd from hence.
Cancel his bond of life, dear God, I pray,
That I may live and say 'The dog is dead'.

Queen Elizabeth

O, thou didst prophesy the time would come
That I should wish for thee to help me curse
That bottled spider, that foul bunch-back'd toad!

Queen Margaret

I call'd thee then vain flourish of my fortune;
I call'd thee then poor shadow, painted queen,
The presentation of but what I was,
The flattering index of a direful pageant,
One heav'd a-high to be hurl'd down below,
A mother only mock'd with two fair babes,
A dream of what thou wast, a garish flag
To be the aim of every dangerous shot,
A sign of dignity, a breath, a bubble,
A queen in jest, only to fill the scene.
Where is thy husband now? Where be thy brothers?
Where be thy two sons? Wherein dost thou joy?
Who sues, and kneels, and says 'God save the Queen'?
Where be the bending peers that flattered thee?
Where be the thronging troops that followed thee?
Decline all this, and see what now thou art:
For happy wife, a most distressed widow;
For joyful mother, one that wails the name;
For one being su'd to, one that humbly sues;
For Queen, a very caitiff crown'd with care;
For she that scorn'd at me, now scorn'd of me;
For she being fear'd of all, now fearing one;
For she commanding all, obey'd of none.
Thus hath the course of justice whirl'd about
And left thee but a very prey to time,
Having no more but thought of what thou wast
To torture thee the more, being what thou art.

110. *the just proportion:* your fair share.

111. *burden'd yoke:* weighty burden. A *yoke* is a piece of harness worn on the neck or shoulders of animals to enable them to pull a load.

114. *mischance:* unhappy experience.

118. *Forbear to sleep:* stop yourself from sleeping.
fast: go without food.

122. *Bett'ring thy loss:* making what you have lost seem better than it was.

123. *Revolving:* turning over in your mind.

124. *quicken them:* make them come to life.

126. The Duchess asks a question that may be in the audience's mind: 'what's the point of talking about our unhappiness?'

128. 'Since her joys are dead and have left nothing behind them to pass on to others, her empty words are all she has.'

130-1. 'Let them be free to do as they like. Although what they say will not help in any other way, at least they will relieve her grief.'

135. *be . . . exclaims:* Let your cries and curses (against Richard) flow freely.

Thou didst usurp my place, and dost thou not
Usurp the just proportion of my sorrow?
Now thy proud neck bears half my burden'd yoke,
From which even here I slip my weary head
And leave the burden of it all on thee.
Farewell, York's wife, and queen of sad mischance;
These English woes shall make me smile in France.

Queen Elizabeth

O thou well skill'd in curses, stay awhile
And teach me how to curse mine enemies!

Queen Margaret

Forbear to sleep the nights, and fast the days;
Compare dead happiness with living woe;
Think that thy babes were sweeter than they were,
And he that slew them fouler than he is.
Bett'ring thy loss makes the bad-causer worse;
Revolving this will teach thee how to curse.

Queen Elizabeth

My words are dull; O, quicken them with thine!

Queen Margaret

Thy woes will make them sharp and pierce like mine.

Exit

Duchess of York

Why should calamity be full of words?

Queen Elizabeth

Windy attorneys to their client woes,
Airy succeeders of intestate joys,
Poor breathing orators of miseries,
Let them have scope; though what they will impart
Help nothing else, yet do they ease the heart.

Duchess of York

If so, then be not tongue-tied. Go with me,
And in the breath of bitter words let's smother
My damned son that thy two sweet sons smother'd.
The trumpet sounds; be copious in exclaims.

136. *expedition:* Richard is marching against Buckingham.

141. *branded:* burned with a hot iron as a means of identification Criminals were sometimes branded as part of their punishment.
142. *ow'd:* owned.

149-51. Richard's order suggests that he is angered and stung by these accusations. To blot them out is not as subtle a way of dealing with them as he might have used at other times; but he does not need to trick anyone any more.
151. *the Lord's anointed:* The king was believed to be God's deputy on earth, and to rule on his behalf.

152. *entreat me fair:* treat me with respect.

156. This answer lacks the respect for her that she is trying to appeal to.

Enter KING RICHARD *and his* TRAIN, *marching with drums and trumpets*

King Richard
Who intercepts me in my expedition?

Duchess of York
O, she that might have intercepted thee,
By strangling thee in her accursed womb,
From all the slaughters, wretch, that thou hast done!

Queen Elizabeth
Hidest thou that forehead with a golden crown
Where't should be branded, if that right were right,
The slaughter of the Prince that ow'd that crown,
And the dire death of my poor sons and brothers?
Tell me, thou villain slave, where are my children?

Duchess of York
Thou toad, thou toad, where is thy brother Clarence?
And little Ned Plantagenet, his son?

Queen Elizabeth
Where is the gentle Rivers, Vaughan, Grey?

Duchess of York
Where is kind Hastings?

King Richard
A flourish, trumpets! Strike alarum, drums!
Let not the heavens hear these tell-tale women
Rail on the Lord's anointed. Strike, I say!

Flourish. Alarums

Either be patient and entreat me fair,
Or with the clamorous report of war
Thus will I drown your exclamations.

Duchess of York
Art thou my son?

King Richard
Ay, I thank God, my father, and yourself.

Duchess of York
Then patiently hear my impatience.

158. *your condition:* She is impatient.

159. *brook . . . reproof:* tolerate criticism.

163. *stay'd:* waited.
164. *torment and agony:* the pains of labour at his birth.

169. *tetchy:* bad-tempered.
wayward: awkward.

172. *Thy age confirm'd:* your maturity, when your character wa established.
173. *More mild:* less fierce (than when young).
harmful-kind: apparently kind, but really evil.

176. No one has been able to explain the reference to Humphrey Hou satisfactorily.

178. *disgracious in:* unpleasing to.

King Richard

Madam, I have a touch of your condition
That cannot brook the accent of reproof.

Duchess of York

O, let me speak!

King Richard Do, then; but I'll not hear.

Duchess of York

I will be mild and gentle in my words.

King Richard

And brief, good mother; for I am in haste.

Duchess of York

Art thou so hasty? I have stay'd for thee,
God knows, in torment and in agony.

King Richard

And came I not at last to comfort you?

Duchess of York

No, by the holy rood, thou know'st it well
Thou cam'st on earth to make the earth my hell.
A grievous burden was thy birth to me;
Tetchy and wayward was thy infancy;
Thy school-days frightful, desp'rate, wild, and furious;
Thy prime of manhood daring, bold, and venturous;
Thy age confirm'd, proud, subtle, sly, and bloody,
More mild, but yet more harmful-kind in hatred.
What comfortable hour canst thou name
That ever grac'd me with thy company?

King Richard

Faith, none but Humphrey Hour, that call'd your Grace
To breakfast once forth of my company.
If I be so disgracious in your eye,
Let me march on and not offend you, madam.
Strike up the drum.

Duchess of York I prithee hear me speak.

King Richard

You speak too bitterly.

183. 'All right. On that condition.'

184. *ordinance:* law.

185. *turn:* return.

189. *tire:* There are three meanings here: (1) cover like a dress, as in 'attire'; (2) make tired; (3) prey upon.

191. *adverse:* opposing.

193. *Whisper:* whisper to.

196. *Shame . . . life:* Throughout your life you have behaved shamefully.
attend: A pun: (1) wait for; (2) serve.

199. Once again, as in Act I, Scene ii, Richard begins wooing at time when he is being cursed.

200. *moe:* more.

203. *level:* aim.

208. She is prepared to say that her daughter is a bastard.

Duchess of York Hear me a word;
For I shall never speak to thee again.

King Richard
So.

Duchess of York
Either thou wilt die by God's just ordinance
Ere from this war thou turn a conqueror;
Or I with grief and extreme age shall perish
And never more behold thy face again.
Therefore take with thee my most grievous curse,
Which in the day of battle tire thee more
Than all the complete armour that thou wear'st!
My prayers on the adverse party fight;
And there the little souls of Edward's children
Whisper the spirits of thine enemies
And promise them success and victory.
Bloody thou art; bloody will be thy end.
Shame serves thy life and doth thy death attend.

Exit

Queen Elizabeth
Though far more cause, yet much less spirit to curse.
Abides in me; I say amen to her.

King Richard
Stay, madam, I must talk a word with you.

Queen Elizabeth
I have no moe sons of the royal blood
For thee to slaughter. For my daughters, Richard,
They shall be praying nuns, not weeping queens;
And therefore level not to hit their lives.

King Richard
You have a daughter call'd Elizabeth.
Virtuous and fair, royal and gracious.

Queen Elizabeth
And must she die for this? O, let her live,
And I'll corrupt her manners, stain her beauty,
Slander myself as false to Edward's bed,

209. *infamy:* dishonour.

214. Richard is only interested in her because of her closeness to the throne.

216. *good . . . opposite:* Astrologers believe that people's lives are affected by the positions of the planets when they were born. Richard is saying that the princes' deaths were ordained by the stars, and he had little to do with them.

218. 'Men cannot avoid the fate decided for them.'

219. *avoided grace:* She means here that Richard, who has rejected the grace of God, controls the fate of others.

223. *cozen'd:* cheated.

225. *lanc'd:* stabbed.

230. *still use:* repeated indulgence in.

Throw over her the veil of infamy;
So she may live unscarr'd of bleeding slaughter,
I will confess she was not Edward's daughter.

King Richard

Wrong not her birth; she is a royal Princess.

Queen Elizabeth

To save her life I'll say she is not so.

King Richard

Her life is safest only in her birth.

Queen Elizabeth

And only in that safety died her brothers.

King Richard

Lo, at their birth good stars were opposite.

Queen Elizabeth

No, to their lives ill friends were contrary.

King Richard

All unavoided is the doom of destiny.

Queen Elizabeth

True, when avoided grace makes destiny.
My babes were destin'd to a fairer death,
If grace had bless'd thee with a fairer life.

King Richard

You speak as if that I had slain my cousins.

Queen Elizabeth

Cousins, indeed; and by their uncle cozen'd
Of comfort, kingdom, kindred, freedom, life.
Whose hand soever lanc'd their tender hearts,
Thy head, all indirectly, gave direction.
No doubt the murd'rous knife was dull and blunt
Till it was whetted on thy stone-hard heart
To revel in the entrails of my lambs.
But that still use of grief makes wild grief tame,
My tongue should to thy ears not name my boys
Till that my nails were anchor'd in thine eyes;
And I, in such a desp'rate bay of death,
Like a poor bark, of sails and tackling reft,
Rush all to pieces on thy rocky bosom.

236. *so thrive I:* may I so prosper.

237. *success:* outcome.

247-8. We must remember that Queen Margaret has just reminded her of the uncertainty of these things.

248. *demise:* a legal term meaning 'transmit'. Here it suggests that Richard's claim is illegal.

251-3. 'If you will forget the anger and grief that you feel at the wrong which you think I have done to you.'
Lethe: the river of forgetfulness. In ancient Greek legend, someone who drank the water from the river, or was immersed in it, forgot all his earlier life.

254. *process . . . kindness:* the story of the kindness you intend to do

255. *thy kindness' date:* the length of time your kindness lasts.

256. *from:* Elizabeth takes this to mean 'not in agreement with'. She gives it the same meaning in lines 259 and 260.

257. *My daughter's mother:* Elizabeth, who knows Richard well.
with her soul: We should say, 'with all her heart'.

King Richard

Madam, so thrive I in my enterprise
And dangerous success of bloody wars,
As I intend more good to you or yours
Than ever you or yours by me were harm'd!

Queen Elizabeth

What good is cover'd with the face of heaven,
To be discover'd, that can do me good?

King Richard

Th' advancement of your children, gentle lady.

Queen Elizabeth

Up to some scaffold, there to lose their heads?

King Richard

Unto the dignity and height of Fortune,
The high imperial type of this earth's glory.

Queen Elizabeth

Flatter my sorrow with report of it;
Tell me what state, what dignity, what honour,
Canst thou demise to any child of mine?

King Richard

Even all I have—ay, and myself and all
Will I withal endow a child of thine;
So in the Lethe of thy angry soul
Thou drown the sad remembrance of those wrongs
Which thou supposest I have done to thee.

Queen Elizabeth

Be brief, lest that the process of thy kindness
Last longer telling than thy kindness' date.

King Richard

Then know, that from my soul I love thy daughter.

Queen Elizabeth

My daughter's mother thinks it with her soul.

King Richard

What do you think?

Queen Elizabeth

That thou dost love my daughter from thy soul.
So from thy soul's love didst thou love her brothers,

262. *confound:* twist.

265. This is Queen Elizabeth's way of saying that she will never allow her daughter to marry Richard.

270. *humour:* temperament, nature.

274. *haply:* perhaps.

275-6. After the battle of Towton, Margaret gave Richard, Duke of York, a cloth soaked in the blood of his son, Rutland.

275. *Therefore:* for the same purpose.

sometimes: on one occasion.

278. *purple sap:* blood.

And from my heart's love I do thank thee for it.

King Richard

Be not so hasty to confound my meaning.
I mean that with my soul I love thy daughter
And do intend to make her Queen of England.

Queen Elizabeth

Well, then, who dost thou mean shall be her king?

King Richard

Even he that makes her Queen. Who else should be?

Queen Elizabeth

What, thou?

King Richard

Even so. How think you of it?

Queen Elizabeth

How canst thou woo her?

King Richard That would I learn of you,
As one being best acquainted with her humour.

Queen Elizabeth

And wilt thou learn of me?

King Richard Madam, with all my heart.

Queen Elizabeth

Send to her, by the man that slew her brothers,
A pair of bleeding hearts; thereon engrave
'Edward' and 'York'. Then haply will she weep;
Therefore present to her—as sometime Margaret
Did to thy father, steep'd in Rutland's blood—
A handkerchief; which, say to her, did drain
The purple sap from her sweet brother's body,
And bid her wipe her weeping eyes withal.
If this inducement move her not to love,
Send her a letter of thy noble deeds;
Tell her thou mad'st away her uncle Clarence,
Her uncle Rivers; ay, and for her sake
Mad'st quick conveyance with her good aunt Anne.

King Richard

You mock me, madam; this is not the way
To win your daughter.

287-8. Richard's reputation makes his task impossible. That even he realizes that he has given himself a task that is too difficult is perhaps implied by the feebleness of his answer in lines 285-6. His strength seems to have deserted him as he faces the truth about himself. If this is so, then the way he lets Queen Elizabeth cheat him into believing that she has been persuaded by him, later in this scene, must be the result of wishful thinking. To hear what her real intention is we have to wait until Act IV, Scene v, lines 7-8.

291. *bloody spoil:* murderous destruction.

292-337. Richard's appeal to reason implies that he thinks that others feel as little as he does; that ambition is their only motive.

292. *Look what:* whatever.

amended: put right.

293. Richard's understatement takes our breath away. Do you think he speaks like this deliberately, as he used to, or has he lost his touch?

shall deal unadvisedly: are bound to behave unwisely.

298. *quicken your increase:* make sure you have descendants.

301. *doating:* fond.

303. *of your metal:* with the same spirit and qualities.

304-5. 'All the result of the same effort, except that your daughter will have to suffer a night of groans in labour. But you suffered in the same way at her birth.'

Queen Elizabeth There is no other way;
Unless thou couldst put on some other shape
And not be Richard that hath done all this.
King Richard
Say that I did all this for love of her.
Queen Elizabeth
Nay, then indeed she cannot choose but hate thee,
Having bought love with such a bloody spoil.
King Richard
Look what is done cannot be now amended.
Men shall deal unadvisedly sometimes,
Which after-hours gives leisure to repent.
If I did take the kingdom from your sons,
To make amends I'll give it to your daughter.
If I have kill'd the issue of your womb,
To quicken your increase I will beget
Mine issue of your blood upon your daughter.
A grandam's name is little less in love
Than is the doating title of a mother;
They are as children but one step below,
Even of your metal, of your very blood;
Of all one pain, save for a night of groans
Endur'd of her, for whom you bid like sorrow.
Your children were vexation to your youth;
But mine shall be a comfort to your age.
The loss you have is but a son being King,
And by that loss your daughter is made Queen.
I cannot make you what amends I would,
Therefore accept such kindness as I can.
Dorset your son, that with a fearful soul
Leads discontented steps in foreign soil,
This fair alliance quickly shall call home
To high promotions and great dignity.
The King, that calls your beauteous daughter wife,
Familiarly shall call thy Dorset brother;
Again shall you be mother to a king,
And all the ruins of distressful times

323. *orient:* particularly shining.

329. *aspiring:* hopeful, ambitious.

337. *Caesar's Caesar:* She shall rule over a king.

338. *father's brother:* Richard and Elizabeth's daughter are too closely related for the marriage to be acceptable to the church.

344. 'Say that this marriage will make peace certain in this country.'

345. *still-lasting:* She means that Richard and his wife would always be fighting each other.

346. *entreats:* begs.

347. *King's King:* God.

Repair'd with double riches of content.
What! we have many goodly days to see.
The liquid drops of tears that you have shed
Shall come again, transform'd to orient pearl,
Advantaging their loan with interest
Of ten times double gain of happiness.
Go, then, my mother, to thy daughter go;
Make bold her bashful years with your experience;
Prepare her ears to hear a wooer's tale;
Put in her tender heart th' aspiring flame
Of golden sovereignty; acquaint the Princess
With the sweet silent hours of marriage joys.
And when this arm of mine hath chastised
The petty rebel, dull-brain'd Buckingham,
Bound with triumphant garlands will I come,
And lead thy daughter to a conqueror's bed;
To whom I will retail my conquest won,
And she shall be sole victoress, Caesar's Caesar.

Queen Elizabeth

What were I best to say? Her father's brother
Would be her lord? Or shall I say her uncle?
Or he that slew her brothers and her uncles?
Under what title shall I woo for thee
That God, the law, my honour, and her love
Can make seem pleasing to her tender years?

King Richard

Infer fair England's peace by this alliance.

Queen Elizabeth

Which she shall purchase with still-lasting war.

King Richard

Tell her the King, that may command, entreats.

Queen Elizabeth

That at her hands which the King's King forbids.

King Richard

Say she shall be a high and mighty queen.

Queen Elizabeth

To wail the title, as her mother doth.

353. *fairly:* happily.

356. *subject:* someone she will be able to rule.

362. *shallow:* not convincing.
quick: glib.

363. *dead:* This is the opposite of 'quick' when it means 'living'.

367. The Order of St George and the Order of the Garter were th country's highest orders of chivalry. Richard was a knight of both
368. *Profan'd:* Richard has brought dishonour on a sacred order, th Order of St George.

King Richard
Say I will love her everlastingly.
Queen Elizabeth
But how long shall that title 'ever' last?
King Richard
Sweetly in force unto her fair life's end.
Queen Elizabeth
But how long fairly shall her sweet life last?
King Richard
As long as heaven and nature lengthens it.
Queen Elizabeth
As long as hell and Richard likes of it.
King Richard
Say I, her sovereign, am her subject low.
Queen Elizabeth
But she, your subject, loathes such sovereignty.
King Richard
Be eloquent in my behalf to her.
Queen Elizabeth
An honest tale speeds best being plainly told.
King Richard
Then plainly to her tell my loving tale.
Queen Elizabeth
Plain and not honest is too harsh a style.
King Richard
Your reasons are too shallow and too quick.
Queen Elizabeth
O, no, my reasons are too deep and dead—
Too deep and dead, poor infants, in their graves.
King Richard
Harp not on that string, madam; that is past.
Queen Elizabeth
Harp on it still shall I till heartstrings break.
King Richard
Now, by my George, my garter, and my crown—
Queen Elizabeth
Profan'd, dishonour'd, and the third usurp'd.

371. *pawn'd:* given up.
virtue: quality.

375-8. Richard is struggling harder here than he has ever had to struggle before.

380. She refers to the reconciliation made in Act II, Scene i.

382. *Him:* God.

391. *Hereafter time:* the time to come.
392. *The children:* Perhaps she means Clarence's children.
393. *Ungovern'd youth:* children without a father to guide them.
in their age: when they grow older.

King Richard
I swear—
Queen Elizabeth By nothing; for this is no oath:
Thy George, profan'd, hath lost his lordly honour;
Thy garter, blemish'd, pawn'd his knightly virtue;
Thy crown, usurp'd, disgrac'd his kingly glory.
If something thou wouldst swear to be believ'd,
Swear then by something that thou hast not wrong'd.
King Richard
Then, by my self—
Queen Elizabeth Thy self is self-misus'd.
King Richard
Now, by the world—
Queen Elizabeth 'Tis full of thy foul wrongs.
King Richard
My father's death—
Queen Elizabeth Thy life hath it dishonour'd.
King Richard
Why, then, by God—
Queen Elizabeth God's wrong is most of all.
If thou didst fear to break an oath with Him,
The unity the King my husband made
Thou hadst not broken, nor my brothers died.
If thou hadst fear'd to break an oath by Him,
Th' imperial metal, circling now thy head,
Had grac'd the tender temples of my child;
And both the Princes had been breathing here,
Which now, two tender bedfellows for dust,
Thy broken faith hath made the prey for worms.
What canst thou swear by now?
King Richard The time to come.
Queen Elizabeth
That thou hast wronged in the time o'erpast;
For I myself have many tears to wash
Hereafter time, for time past wrong'd by thee.
The children live whose fathers thou hast slaughter'd,
Ungovern'd youth, to wail it in their age;

395. *with their age:* as well as their old age.

397. *ere:* before.
by times . . . o'erpast: by the times that you have already lived through and ruined.

400-6. Richard is becoming desperate in what he says.
400. *Myself . . . confound!* May I cheat myself with my own tricks.
401. *bar:* deny.

403. 'May all favourable stars withdraw their influence.'

405. *immaculate:* pure.
406. *tender:* care for.

411. 'The marriage and my happiness can only be prevented if you are prepared to see ruin come upon us all.'
412. The idea is now changed to a threat: 'If we do not marry, ruin will certainly follow.'
414. *attorney:* spokesman.

416. *my deserts:* what I deserve for my behaviour up to now.

418. *peevish-fond:* foolishly spiteful.

421. 'Shall I forget that I am a grieving mother, so that I can be the queen mother?'

422. 'Yes, if thinking of yourself in one way does your other self harm.'

The parents live whose children thou hast butcher'd,
Old barren plants, to wail it with their age.
Swear not by time to come; for that thou hast
Misus'd ere us'd, by times ill-us'd o'erpast.

King Richard

As I intend to prosper and repent,
So thrive I in my dangerous affairs
Of hostile arms! Myself myself confound!
Heaven and fortune bar me happy hours!
Day, yield me not thy light; nor, night, thy rest!
Be opposite all planets of good luck
To my proceeding!—if, with dear heart's love,
Immaculate devotion, holy thoughts,
I tender not thy beauteous princely daughter.
In her consists my happiness and thine;
Without her, follows to myself and thee,
Herself, the land, and many a Christian soul,
Death, desolation, ruin, and decay.
It cannot be avoided but by this;
It will not be avoided but by this.
Therefore, dear mother—I must call you so—
Be the attorney of my love to her;
Plead what I will be, not what I have been;
Not my deserts, but what I will deserve.
Urge the necessity and state of times,
And be not peevish-fond in great designs.

Queen Elizabeth

Shall I be tempted of the devil thus?

King Richard

Ay, if the devil tempt you to do good.

Queen Elizabeth

Shall I forget myself to be myself?

King Richard

Ay, if your self's remembrance wrong yourself.

Queen Elizabeth

Yet thou didst kill my children.

425-6. *Where . . . themselves:* The Phoenix, a fabulous and unique Arabian bird, reproduced itself by being burnt on a nest of spices, rising, a new bird, from the flames. Richard says that his own and the princess Elizabeth's children will console Queen Elizabeth for the deaths of her other children.
426. *recomforture:* comfort, consolation.

429-30. Either Elizabeth has really been persuaded, or, as seems more likely, she is playing her part thoroughly—as Richard himself usually does—and putting in the convincing touches.

432. Richard has lost his skill in judgement.

435-541. Historically, there was a gap of two years between Buckingham's rising and Richmond's successful invasion.
435. *puissant:* powerful.
to our shores: They are going to oppose, though only half-heartedly, the invading fleet.
436. *hollow-hearted:* insincere, lacking in determination.
438. *their admiral:* i.e. in command of the ships.
439. *hull:* lie waiting.

445. *Post:* hurry.

King Richard
But in your daughter's womb I bury them;
Where, in that nest of spicery, they will breed
Selves of themselves, to your recomforture.

Queen Elizabeth
Shall I go win my daughter to thy will?

King Richard
And be a happy mother by the deed.

Queen Elizabeth
I go. Write to me very shortly,
And you shall understand from me her mind.

King Richard
Bear her my true love's kiss; and so, farewell.

Kissing her. Exit QUEEN ELIZABETH

Relenting fool, and shallow, changing woman!

Enter RATCLIFF; CATESBY *following*

How now! what news?

Ratcliff
Most mighty sovereign, on the western coast
Rideth a puissant navy; to our shores
Throng many doubtful hollow-hearted friends,
Unarm'd, and unresolv'd to beat them back.
'Tis thought that Richmond is their admiral;
And there they hull, expecting but the aid
Of Buckingham to welcome them ashore.

King Richard
Some light-foot friend post to the Duke of Norfolk.
Ratcliff, thyself—or Catesby; where is he?

Catesby
Here, my good lord.

King Richard Catesby, fly to the Duke.

Catesby
I will, my lord, with all convenient haste.

King Richard
Ratcliff, come hither. Post to Salisbury;

448-9. Richard's forgetfulness is another sign that he is losing his touch.

450. *levy:* raise.
straight: immediately.

452. *suddenly:* immediately.

460-3. Richard's irritation springs from his general anxiety and from his fear that Stanley will be disloyal.

465. *white-liver'd runagate:* cowardly traitor.

When thou com'st thither—[*To* CATESBY] Dull,
unmindful villain,
Why stay'st thou here, and go'st not to the Duke?

Catesby
First, mighty liege, tell me your Highness' pleasure,
What from your Grace I shall deliver to him.

King Richard
O, true, good Catesby. Bid him levy straight
The greatest strength and power that he can make
And meet me suddenly at Salisbury.

Catesby
I go.

Exit

Ratcliff
What, may it please you, shall I do at Salisbury?

King Richard
Why, what wouldst thou do there before I go?

Ratcliff
Your Highness told me I should post before.

King Richard
My mind is chang'd.

Enter LORD STANLEY

Stanley, what news with you?

Stanley
None good, my liege, to please you with the hearing;
Nor none so bad but well may be reported.

King Richard
Hoyday, a riddle! neither good nor bad!
What need'st thou run so many miles about,
When thou mayest tell thy tale the nearest way?
Once more, what news?

Stanley Richmond is on the seas.

King Richard
There let him sink, and be the seas on him!
White-liver'd runagate, what doth he there?

470. *chair:* throne.
unsway'd: not held firmly.

473. *great York:* Edmund, Duke of York, son of Edward III.

474. *what makes he:* what he is doing.

476. *Unless for that:* We should say simply, 'unless'.

477. *wherefore:* why.
the Welshman: Richmond was a member of a Welsh family, the Tudors.

480. *power:* army.

481. *thy tennants . . . followers:* These were the people who should make up part of Richard's army.

484. *in the north:* The Stanley lands were in Cheshire and Lancashire.

488. *Pleaseth:* if it please.

Stanley
I know not, mighty sovereign, but by guess.
King Richard
Well, as you guess?
Stanley
Stirr'd up by Dorset, Buckingham, and Morton,
He makes for England here to claim the crown.
King Richard
Is the chair empty? Is the sword unsway'd?
Is the King dead, the empire unpossess'd?
What heir of York is there alive but we?
And who is England's King but great York's heir?
Then tell me what makes he upon the seas.
Stanley
Unless for that, my liege, I cannot guess.
King Richard
Unless for that he comes to be your liege,
You cannot guess wherefore the Welshman comes.
Thou wilt revolt and fly to him, I fear.
Stanley
No, my good lord; therefore mistrust me not.
King Richard
Where is thy power then, to beat him back?
Where be thy tenants and thy followers?
Are they not now upon the western shore,
Safe-conducting the rebels from their ships?
Stanley
No, my good lord, my friends are in the north.
King Richard
Cold friends to me. What do they in the north,
When they should serve their sovereign in the west?
Stanley
They have not been commanded, mighty King.
Pleaseth your Majesty to give me leave,
I'll muster up my friends and meet your Grace
Where and what time your Majesty shall please.

497. *his head's . . . frail:* he has little chance of escaping execution.

500. *advertised:* informed.

505. *competitors:* allies, friends who will fight on their side.

508. The hooting of owls was thought to be the signal of a coming death. This outburst marks a complete, but temporary, loss of control by Richard.

King Richard

Ay, ay, thou wouldst be gone to join with Richmond;
But I'll not trust thee.

Stanley Most mighty sovereign,
You have no cause to hold my friendship doubtful.
I never was nor never will be false.

King Richard

Go, then, and muster men. But leave behind
Your son, George Stanley. Look your heart be firm,
Or else his head's assurance is but frail.

Stanley

So deal with him as I prove true to you.

Exit. Enter a MESSENGER

Messenger

My gracious sovereign, now in Devonshire,
As I by friends am well advertised,
Sir Edward Courtney and the haughty prelate,
Bishop of Exeter, his elder brother,
With many moe confederates, are in arms.

Enter another MESSENGER

Second Messenger

In Kent, my liege, the Guilfords are in arms;
And every hour more competitors
Flock to the rebels, and their power grows strong.

Enter another MESSENGER

Third Messenger

My lord, the army of great Buckingham—

King Richard

Out on you, owls! Nothing but songs of death?

He strikes him

There, take thou that till thou bring better news.

Third Messenger

The news I have to tell your Majesty

514. *mercy:* pardon.

516. *well-advised:* thoughtful and practical.

527. *Upon his party:* in his interest, on his behalf.
528. *Hois'd:* hoisted.

534. *Milford:* Milford Haven in south-west Wales.

536. *Salisbury:* in southern England.
537. *royal battle:* a battle that decides who shall be king.

Is that by sudden floods and fall of waters
Buckingham's army is dispers'd and scatter'd;
And he himself wander'd away alone,
No man knows whither.

King Richard I cry thee mercy.
There is my purse to cure that blow of thine.
Hath any well-advised friend proclaim'd
Reward to him that brings the traitor in?

Third Messenger
Such proclamation hath been made, my lord.

Enter another MESSENGER

Fourth Messenger
Sir Thomas Lovel and Lord Marquis Dorset,
'Tis said, my liege, in Yorkshire are in arms.
But this good comfort bring I to your Highness—
The Britaine navy is dispers'd by tempest.
Richmond in Dorsetshire sent out a boat
Unto the shore, to ask those on the banks
If they were his assistants, yea or no;
Who answer'd him they came from Buckingham
Upon his party. He, mistrusting them,
Hois'd sail, and made his course again for Britaine.

King Richard
March on, march on, since we are up in arms;
If not to fight with foreign enemies,
Yet to beat down these rebels here at home.

Re-enter CATESBY

Catesby
My liege, the Duke of Buckingham is taken—
That is the best news. That the Earl of Richmond
Is with a mighty power landed at Milford
Is colder tidings, yet they must be told.

King Richard
Away towards Salisbury! While we reason here
A royal battle might be won and lost.

SCENE V

2. *boar:* Richard. A boar was his emblem.
3. *frank'd . . . hold:* shut in prison.

5. 'Because I am afraid this will happen, I am keeping back my help at the moment.'

8. *espouse:* marry.

10. *Ha'rford West:* Haverford West, in south-west Wales.

11. *of name:* of good reputation, well-known.

14. *redoubted:* valiant, courageous.
Pembroke: Jasper Tudor, Richmond's uncle.

17. *bend:* direct.
18. *by the way:* on the way.

19. *hie thee:* hurry.
20. *resolve . . . mind:* Clear up his doubts about what I want to do.

Some one take order Buckingham be brought
To Salisbury; the rest march on with me.

Flourish. Exeunt

SCENE V—*Lord Derby's house*

Enter STANLEY *and* SIR CHRISTOPHER URSWICK

Stanley

Sir Christopher, tell Richmond this from me:
That in the sty of the most deadly boar
My son George Stanley is frank'd up in hold;
If I revolt, off goes young George's head;
The fear of that holds off my present aid.
So, get thee gone; commend me to thy lord.
Withal say that the Queen hath heartily consented
He should espouse Elizabeth her daughter.
But tell me, where is princely Richmond now?

Urswick

At Pembroke, or at Ha'rford west in Wales.

Stanley

What men of name resort to him?

Urswick

Sir Walter Herbert, a renowned soldier;
Sir Gilbert Talbot, Sir William Stanley,
Oxford, redoubted Pembroke, Sir James Blunt,
And Rice ap Thomas, with a valiant crew;
And many other of great name and worth;
And towards London do they bend their power,
If by the way they be not fought withal.

Stanley

Well, hie thee to thy lord; I kiss his hand;
My letter will resolve him of my mind.
Farewell.

Exeunt

ACT FIVE

SCENE I

In this scene we see the fulfilment of more of the oaths and the filling in of the pattern of punishment. With each of these episodes we feel that justice is coming closer to Richard himself.

5. *miscarried:* been treated unjustly.

6. *underhand:* dishonest.

10. *All-Souls' day:* a day in the calendar of the Christian church, 2n November, when those who have died as Christians are remembere

12. *doomsday:* the day it meets its fate.

13. *in King Edward's time:* He means at the reconciliation in Act I Scene i.

19. 'Is the time fixed for me to be punished, after I have been allow to get away with my crimes for so long.'
20. *high All-Seer:* God, who sees all and cannot be cheated.
21. *feigned:* false. He did not mean what he said.
22. *in earnest:* seriously.

ACT FIVE

SCENE I—*Salisbury. An open place*

Enter the SHERIFF *and* GUARD, *with* BUCKINGHAM, *led to execution*

Buckingham

Will not King Richard let me speak with him?

Sheriff

No, my good lord; therefore be patient.

Buckingham

Hastings, and Edward's children, Grey, and Rivers,
Holy King Henry, and thy fair son Edward,
Vaughan, and all that have miscarried
By underhand corrupted foul injustice,
If that your moody discontented souls
Do through the clouds behold this present hour,
Even for revenge mock my destruction!
This is All-Souls' day, fellow, is it not?

Sheriff

It is, my lord.

Buckingham

Why, then All-Souls' day is my body's doomsday.
This is the day which in King Edward's time
I wish'd might fall on me when I was found
False to his children and his wife's allies;
This is the day wherein I wish'd to fall
By the false faith of him whom most I trusted;
This, this All-Souls' day to my fearful soul
Is the determin'd respite of my wrongs;
That high All-Seer which I dallied with
Hath turn'd my feigned prayer on my head
And given in earnest what I begg'd in jest.

24. *their masters' bosoms:* the breasts of owners of the swords.

25. *on my neck:* i.e. where the axe will strike him.

29. So Buckingham cannot complain; he is being justly rewarded.

SCENE II

Stage Direction. *Tamworth* is in Leicestershire, in the English Midlands *colours:* the banners under which the different units in the army fought

1. *Fellows in arms:* fellow-soldiers.

3. *bowels . . . land:* We should say, the heart of the country.

4. *impediment:* hindrance, obstruction.

5. *we:* Richmond is already speaking like a king.

6. *Lines:* He is referring to Stanley's letter that we heard about i Act IV, Scene v.

7-10. Richmond makes full, colourful and contemptuous use o Richard's emblem.

9. *Swills:* gulps down.
wash: kitchen waste mixed with water, that is fed to pigs.

10. *embowell'd bosoms:* disembowelled bodies. ('bosoms' is used t suggest greater sensitiveness to pain.)

16. *sharp:* fierce and painful.

17. 'Every man's sense of injustice makes him as strong as a thousan men.'

18. *homicide:* murderer.

Thus doth He force the swords of wicked men
To turn their own points in their masters' bosoms.
Thus Margaret's curse falls heavy on my neck.
'When he' quoth she 'shall split thy heart with sorrow,
Remember Margaret was a prophetess.'
Come lead me, officers, to the block of shame;
Wrong hath but wrong, and blame the due of blame.

Exeunt

SCENE II—*Camp near Tamworth*

Enter RICHMOND, OXFORD, SIR JAMES BLUNT, SIR WALTER HERBERT *and* OTHERS, *with drum and colours*

Richmond

Fellows in arms, and my most loving friends,
Bruis'd underneath the yoke of tyranny,
Thus far into the bowels of the land
Have we march'd on without impediment;
And here receive we from our father Stanley
Lines of fair comfort and encouragement.
The wretched, bloody, and usurping boar,
That spoil'd your summer fields and fruitful vines,
Swills your warm blood like wash, and makes his trough
In your embowell'd bosoms—this foul swine
Is now even in the centre of this isle,
Near to the town of Leicester, as we learn.
From Tamworth thither is but one day's march.
In God's name cheerly on, courageous friends,
To reap the harvest of perpetual peace
By this one bloody trial of sharp war.

Oxford

Every man's conscience is a thousand men,
To fight against this guilty homicide.

20. *for fear:* because they are afraid of him.
21. *in his dearest need:* when he needs them most desperately.

22. *vantage:* advantage.

24. *meaner:* humbler, less important.

SCENE III

The play now moves quickly to its climax in the battle scene. Th audience has the final positions of Richard and Richmond made clear but although right is now clearly seen to be on Richmond's side, ther is little doubt that Richard is the more believable figure. He has th courage to look at his own sins squarely, and great courage at th prospect of the battle and in the battle itself. But to say that Richar is still a human figure is not enough: a king was expected to show almos god-like qualities if he was to be properly revered, and Richard lack these virtues.

Since there was no attempt in the Elizabethan theatre to make th stage look like the place in which the actions were happening, it was simple matter to play a scene such as this one. The two opposing armie were represented by the two groups of leaders, each keeping to its ow side of the stage. The ghosts would turn first to Richard and then t Richmond, or would pass from one to the other, and then leave th stage.

Stage Direction. *Bosworth Field* is at Market Bosworth in Leiceste shire.
in arms: in armour.
5. *we . . . knocks:* we cannot avoid a fight. Richard is trying to hel Surrey, who is Norfolk's son, to accept that in a man's world you hav to face up to fighting. Richard, we know, has not only accepted th fact, but enjoyed it.
8. *But . . . tomorrow?* Richard is momentarily not confident that h will win; but he pulls himself together again immediately.
all's . . . that: No good worrying about that now.

9. *descried:* made out, discovered.

Herbert
I doubt not but his friends will turn to us.

Blunt
He hath no friends but what are friends for fear,
Which in his dearest need will fly from him.

Richmond
All for our vantage. Then in God's name march.
True hope is swift and flies with swallow's wings;
Kings it makes gods, and meaner creatures kings.

Exeunt

SCENE III—*Bosworth Field*

Enter KING RICHARD *in arms, with* NORFOLK, RATCLIFF, *the* EARL OF SURREY *and* OTHERS

King Richard
Here pitch our tent, even here in Bosworth field.
My Lord of Surrey, why look you so sad?

Surrey
My heart is ten times lighter than my looks.

King Richard
My Lord of Norfolk!

Norfolk Here, most gracious liege.

King Richard
Norfolk, we must have knocks; ha! must we not?

Norfolk
We must both give and take, my loving lord.

King Richard
Up with my tent! Here will I lie to-night;

Soldiers begin to set up the King's tent

But where to-morrow? Well, all's one for that.
Who hath descried the number of the traitors?

Norfolk
Six or seven thousand is their utmost power.

11. *battalia:* army.

13. *adverse faction:* the enemy side.
want: lack.

15. *survey the vantage:* find positions most favourable to their army.

16. *direction:* knowledge of tactics.

20. *fiery car:* In ancient Greek mythology the sun was a chariot pulled across the sky by horses.

24. *model:* plan.
battle: army drawn up ready for battle.
25. *Limit:* appoint.
several charge: particular duty.
26. *part . . . proportion:* divide in the fairest way.

34. *quarter'd:* encamped.

King Richard
Why, our battalia trebles that account;
Besides, the King's name is a tower of strength,
Which they upon the adverse faction want.
Up with the tent! Come, noble gentlemen,
Let us survey the vantage of the ground.
Call for some men of sound direction.
Let's lack no discipline, make no delay;
For, lords, to-morrow is a busy day.

Exeunt

Enter, on the other side of the Field, RICHMOND, SIR WILLIAM BRANDON, OXFORD, DORSET, *and* OTHERS. *Some pitch Richmond's tent*

Richmond
The weary sun hath made a golden set,
And by the bright tract of his fiery car
Gives token of a goodly day to-morrow.
Sir William Brandon, you shall bear my standard.
Give me some ink and paper in my tent.
I'll draw the form and model of our battle,
Limit each leader to his several charge,
And part in just proportion our small power.
My Lord of Oxford—you, Sir William Brandon—
And you, Sir Walter Herbert—stay with me.
The Earl of Pembroke keeps his regiment;
Good Captain Blunt, bear my good night to him,
And by the second hour in the morning
Desire the Earl to see me in my tent.
Yet one thing more, good Captain, do for me—
Where is Lord Stanley quarter'd, do you know?

Blunt
Unless I have mista'en his colours much—
Which well I am assur'd I have not done—
His regiment lies half a mile at least
South from the mighty power of the King.

Richmond
If without peril it be possible,

40. *make . . . speak:* get in touch.

50. *beaver:* a piece of the helmet that covered the face, and could be raised or lowered.
easier: less stiff.

56. *Stir . . . lark:* be on the move early.

57. *warrant:* promise.

Sweet Blunt, make some good means to speak with him
And give him from me this most needful note.

Blunt

Upon my life, my lord, I'll undertake it;
And so, God give you quiet rest to-night!

Richmond

Good night, good Captain Blunt. Come, gentlemen,
Let us consult upon to-morrow's business.
In to my tent; the dew is raw and cold.

They withdraw into the tent

Enter, to his tent, KING RICHARD, NORFOLK, RATCLIFF *and* CATESBY

King Richard

What is't o'clock?

Catesby It's supper-time, my lord;
It's nine o'clock.

Richmond I will not sup to-night.
Give me some ink and paper.
What, is my beaver easier than it was?
And all my armour laid into my tent?

Catesby

It is, my liege; and all things are in readiness.

King Richard

Good Norfolk, hie thee to thy charge;
Use careful watch, choose trusty sentinels.

Norfolk

I go, my lord.

King Richard

Stir with the lark to-morrow, gentle Norfolk.

Norfolk

I warrant you, my lord.

Exit

King Richard

Catesby!

59. *pursuivant-at-arms:* a junior officer, whose job was to assist the herald in his dealings with the enemy.

63. *watch:* a watch-light, a candle marked off to show how much time has passed while it has been burning.

65. *staves:* the wooden handles of his lances.
sound: strong, uncracked.

70. *cock-shut time:* the time when the cocks settle down for the night.

72. Richard obviously doubts the loyalty of Northumberland.
Give me . . . wine: This is the second time he has asked for it; he may be a little angry or even desperate here.
73. *alacrity of spirit:* light-heartedness, freedom from worry.
74. *was wont to:* usually.
75. *Set it down:* He means the wine.

77. The stage directions indicate that two quite separate scenes are being presented on different parts of the stage.

Catesby
My lord?
King Richard
Send out a pursuivant-at-arms
To Stanley's regiment; bid him bring his power
Before sunrising, lest his son George fall
Into the blind cave of eternal night.

Exit CATESBY

Fill me a bowl of wine. Give me a watch.
Saddle white Surrey for the field to-morrow.
Look that my staves be sound, and not too heavy.
Ratcliff!
Ratcliff
My lord?
King Richard
Saw'st thou the melancholy Lord Northumberland?
Ratcliff
Thomas the Earl of Surrey and himself,
Much about cock-shut time, from troop to troop
Went through the army, cheering up the soldiers.
King Richard
So, I am satisfied. Give me a bowl of wine.
I have not that alacrity of spirit
Nor cheer of mind that I was wont to have.
Set it down. Is ink and paper ready?
Ratcliff
It is, my lord.
King Richard
Bid my guard watch; leave me.
Ratcliff, about the mid of night come to my tent
And help to arm me. Leave me, I say.

Exit RATCLIFF. RICHARD *sleeps*
Enter DERBY *to* RICHMOND *in his tent;* LORDS *attending*

80. *helm:* helmet.

82. *father-in-law:* step-father, husband of his mother.

84. *by attorney:* on her behalf.

87. *flaky:* with streaks of light in it.

88. *season:* time and the affairs associated with it.

90. *arbitrement:* decision.

91. *mortal-staring:* glaring with death in its eyes.

92-3. 'Although I cannot do what I really want to do, I will do my best to hang back and cheat Richard in that way.'

94. *doubtful:* The result is uncertain.

95. *forward:* obviously helpful.

96. *tender:* young.

98. *leisure:* lack of time.

99. *ceremonious vows:* exchanges of affection that are expected on such occasions.

102. *rites:* ceremonies. Stanley regrets that life has become so uncivilized.

103. *speed well!* May things go well for you.

105. *nap:* short sleep.

106. *leaden slumber:* heavy sleep that comes after a sleepless night. *peise:* weigh.

109-18. Richmond is praying. It was customary—in plays at least—for the deserving king, or general, to ask God's help in battle, even if the help should only consist of God's refraining from remembering his faults.

109. *captain:* general, leader of the army.

Derby

Fortune and victory sit on thy helm!

Richmond

All comfort that the dark night can afford
Be to thy person, noble father-in-law!
Tell me, how fares our loving mother?

Derby

I, by attorney, bless thee from thy mother,
Who prays continually for Richmond's good.
So much for that. The silent hours steal on,
And flaky darkness breaks within the east.
In brief, for so the season bids us be,
Prepare thy battle early in the morning,
And put thy fortune to the arbitrement
Of bloody strokes and mortal-staring war.
I, as I may—that which I would I cannot—
With best advantage will deceive the time
And aid thee in this doubtful shock of arms;
But on thy side I may not be too forward,
Lest, being seen, thy brother, tender George,
Be executed in his father's sight.
Farewell; the leisure and the fearful time
Cuts off the ceremonious vows of love
And ample interchange of sweet discourse
Which so-long-sunder'd friends should dwell upon.
God give us leisure for these rites of love!
Once more, adieu; be valiant, and speed well!

Richmond

Good lords, conduct him to his regiment.
I'll strive with troubled thoughts to take a nap,
Lest leaden slumber peise me down to-morrow
When I should mount with wings of victory.
Once more, good night, kind lords and gentlemen.

Exeunt all but RICHMOND

O Thou, whose captain I account myself,
Look on my forces with a gracious eye;

111. *bruising irons:* weapons.

113. *usurping:* Richmond claims that Richard is a usurper because he has taken the throne illegally.
114. *ministers of chastisement:* instruments of God's punishment, even, perhaps, executioners.
116. *watchful:* always on the look-out to do God's will.

Stage Direction. The ghosts appear in the order of their deaths and so recapitulate for us Richard's crimes.

124. *issue:* child.

127. *the Tower:* where Henry was murdered.

133. *fulsome:* cloying, making the drinker feel too full.
134. *guile:* deceitfulness.

136. *fall:* let fall.
edgeless: unable to harm anyone.

Put in their hands Thy bruising irons of wrath,
That they may crush down with a heavy fall
The usurping helmets of our adversaries!
Make us Thy ministers of chastisement,
That we may praise Thee in the victory!
To Thee I do commend my watchful soul
Ere I let fall the windows of mine eyes.
Sleeping and waking, O, defend me still!

Sleeps. Enter the GHOST *of young* PRINCE EDWARD, *son to Henry the Sixth*

Ghost [*To* RICHARD]
Let me sit heavy on thy soul to-morrow!
Think how thou stabb'dst me in my prime of youth
At Tewksbury; despair, therefore, and die!
[*To* RICHMOND] Be cheerful, Richmond; for the wronged souls
Of butcher'd princes fight in thy behalf.
King Henry's issue, Richmond, comforts thee.

Enter the GHOST *of* HENRY THE SIXTH

Ghost [*To* RICHARD]
When I was mortal, my anointed body
By thee was punched full of deadly holes.
Think on the Tower and me. Despair, and die.
Harry the Sixth bids thee despair and die.
[*To* RICHMOND] Virtuous and holy, be thou conqueror!
Harry, that prophesied thou shouldst be King,
Doth comfort thee in thy sleep. Live and flourish!

Enter the GHOST *of* CLARENCE

Ghost [*To* RICHARD]
Let me sit heavy in thy soul to-morrow!
I that was wash'd to death with fulsome wine,
Poor Clarence, by thy guile betray'd to death!
To-morrow in the battle think on me,
And fall thy edgeless sword. Despair and die!

157. *annoy:* harm.
158. Henry VII was the founder of the Tudor dynasty.

[*To* RICHMOND] Thou offspring of the house of Lancaster,
The wronged heirs of York do pray for thee.
Good angels guard thy battle! Live and flourish!

Enter the GHOSTS *of* RIVERS, GREY, *and* VAUGHAN

Rivers [*To* RICHARD]
Let me sit heavy in thy soul to-morrow,
Rivers that died at Pomfret! Despair and die!

Grey [*To* RICHARD]
Think upon Grey, and let thy soul despair!

Vaughan [*To* RICHARD]
Think upon Vaughan, and with guilty fear
Let fall thy lance. Despair and die!

All [*To* RICHMOND]
Awake, and think our wrongs in Richard's bosom
Will conquer him. Awake and win the day.

Enter the GHOST *of* HASTINGS

Ghost [*To* RICHARD]
Bloody and guilty, guiltily awake,
And in a bloody battle end thy days!
Think on Lord Hastings. Despair and die.
[*To* RICHMOND] Quiet untroubled soul, awake, awake!
Arm, fight, and conquer, for fair England's sake!

Enter the GHOSTS *of the two young* PRINCES

Ghosts [*To* RICHARD]
Dream on thy cousins smothered in the Tower.
Let us be lead within thy bosom, Richard,
And weigh thee down to ruin, shame, and death!
Thy nephews' souls bid thee despair and die.
[*To* RICHMOND] Sleep, Richmond, sleep in peace, and wake in joy;
Good angels guard thee from the boar's annoy!
Live, and beget a happy race of kings!
Edward's unhappy sons do bid thee flourish.

Enter the GHOST *of* LADY ANNE, *his wife*

162. *perturbations:* troubles, disturbances.

169. *tyranny:* injustice.

174. *for hope:* for hoping to help you.
177. *in height . . . pride:* Richard is at his height, so his fall, if it comes now, will be great.
178-207. Richard, frightened by the ghosts which he has dreamed of, for the first time really looks at his actions from a different standpoint from his own selfish one. He looks at himself from the outside, and it is a measure of the seriousness of the crisis, as he faces possible death and God's judgement that will follow it, that he hates himself for his crimes. The Richard who delights in his own cleverness and contrasts it with the stupidity of others is gone for ever. Realizing his complete disillusionment we must give full weight to the qualities that he shows in the rest of the action.
178. *Give . . . horse:* Richard is dreaming about the battle, and that his horse has been shot under him. The dream takes up the last idea of Buckingham's ghost and accurately forecasts what will happen.
179. *Have mercy, Jesu!* Richard now dreams that he is dying and is pleading to God for merciful treatment despite all his sins.
181. *The lights burn blue:* It was supposed to be a sign that ghosts were about if flames burned blue.
182. Richard is sweating with fear.
185. *No—yes:* This is the point at which Richard consciously begins to condemn himself.
188-9. *For . . . myself:* Richard, like Margaret and Elizabeth for different reasons, finds his triumph bitter.
188. *Alack:* Alas; an expression of woe or despair. Richard's 'Alas' here suggests that he is at last ashamed of himself; otherwise he would have said '*But* I love myself.'

Ghost [*To* RICHARD]
Richard, thy wife, that wretched Anne thy wife
That never slept a quiet hour with thee
Now fills thy sleep with perturbations.
To-morrow in the battle think on me,
And fall thy edgeless sword. Despair and die.
[*To* RICHMOND] Thou quiet soul, sleep thou a quiet sleep;
Dream of success and happy victory.
Thy adversary's wife doth pray for thee.

Enter the GHOST *of* BUCKINGHAM

Ghost [*To* RICHARD]
The first was I that help'd thee to the crown;
The last was I that felt thy tyranny.
O, in the battle think on Buckingham,
And die in terror of thy guiltiness!
Dream on, dream on of bloody deeds and death;
Fainting, despair; despairing, yield thy breath!
[*To* RICHMOND] I died for hope ere I could lend thee aid;
But cheer thy heart and be thou not dismay'd:
God and good angels fight on Richmond's side;
And Richard falls in height of all his pride.

The GHOSTS *vanish.* RICHARD *starts out of his dream*

King Richard
Give me another horse. Bind up my wounds.
Have mercy, Jesu! Soft! I did but dream.
O coward conscience, how dost thou afflict me!
The lights burn blue. It is now dead midnight.
Cold fearful drops stand on my trembling flesh.
What do I fear? Myself? There's none else by.
Richard loves Richard; that is, I am I.
Is there a murderer here? No—yes, I am.
Then fly. What, from myself? Great reason why—
Lest I revenge. What, myself upon myself!
Alack, I love myself. Wherefore? For any good

192. Remember: 'I am determined to prove a villain.' (Act I, Scene i line 30)
193. The two sides of his nature speak to each other here.
194. *several:* independent.

197. *perjury:* telling lies while on oath.
in . . . degree: of the most serious kind.
198. *stern:* grave, serious.
in . . . degree: of the most frightful kind.
199. 'Every distinct kind of sin, and each one committed to incriminate me in its turn.'
200. *Throng . . . bar:* crowd forward to give evidence (against Richard).

204. *no . . . myself:* Either he sees himself for the evil creature he is, or he means that if he had pity he would have spared himself the distress of getting so deeply into sin.
205-7. These lines seem to be out of place here, and editors presume that they have become misplaced. But it is possible that they are meant to show how Richard's distracted mind switches irrationally from one subject to another.

209. *Zounds:* a mild oath or exclamation which was a corruption of 'God's wounds'. Richard is badly startled, as his exclamation shows.

214. *true:* faithful.

216. *shadows:* illusions.

That I myself have done unto myself?
O, no! Alas, I rather hate myself
For hateful deeds committed by myself!
I am a villain; yet I lie, I am not.
Fool, of thyself speak well. Fool, do not flatter.
My conscience hath a thousand several tongues,
And every tongue brings in a several tale,
And every tale condemns me for a villain.
Perjury, perjury, in the high'st degree;
Murder, stern murder, in the dir'st degree;
All several sins, all us'd in each degree,
Throng to the bar, crying all 'Guilty! guilty!'
I shall despair. There is no creature loves me;
And if I die no soul will pity me:
And wherefore should they, since that I myself
Find in myself no pity to myself?
Methought the souls of all that I had murder'd
Came to my tent, and every one did threat
To-morrow's vengeance on the head of Richard.

Enter RATCLIFF

Ratcliff
My lord!

King Richard
Zounds, who is there?

Ratcliff
Ratcliff, my lord; 'tis I. The early village-cock
Hath twice done salutation to the morn;
Your friends are up and buckle on their armour.

King Richard
O Ratcliff, I have dream'd a fearful dream!
What think'st thou—will our friends prove all true?

Ratcliff
No doubt, my lord.

King Richard O Ratcliff, I fear, I fear.

Ratcliff
Nay, good my lord, be not afraid of shadows.

217. *shadows:* ghosts.

220. *Armed in proof:* dressed in protective armour.

225. *Cry mercy:* I beg your pardon.

226. *tardy sluggard:* someone slow to get up in the morning.

232. *cried on:* spoke of.

233. *jocund:* cheerful.

236. 'About to strike four o'clock.'

237. *direction:* orders.

238. *More . . . said:* If we are to make sense of this speech as it stands, this must mean, 'than I have said in the past'.

239. 'The pressure caused by lack of time.'

King Richard

By the apostle Paul, shadows to-night
Have struck more terror to the soul of Richard
Than can the substance of ten thousand soldiers
Armed in proof and led by shallow Richmond.
'Tis not yet near day. Come, go with me;
Under our tents I'll play the eaves-dropper,
To see if any mean to shrink from me.

Exeunt. Enter the LORDS *to* RICHMOND *sitting in his tent*

Lords

Good morrow, Richmond!

Richmond

Cry mercy, lords and watchful gentlemen,
That you have ta'en a tardy sluggard here.

Lords

How have you slept, my lord?

Richmond

The sweetest sleep and fairest-boding dreams
That ever enter'd in a drowsy head
Have I since your departure had, my lords.
Methought their souls whose bodies Richard murder'd
Came to my tent and cried on victory.
I promise you my soul is very jocund
In the remembrance of so fair a dream.
How far into the morning is it, lords?

Lords

Upon the stroke of four.

Richmond

Why, then 'tis time to arm and give direction.

His Oration to his Soldiers

More than I have said, loving countrymen,
The leisure and enforcement of the time
Forbids to dwell upon; yet remember this:

243. *high-rear'd bulwarks:* protective walls built high in front of us.
244. *Richard except:* with the exception of Richard.

248. 'One who gained his position by murder, and kept it by murder.'

251. *A base . . . stone:* not a precious jewel.
foil: the setting that shows off a jewel.
252. *Set:* A pun: (1) seated; (2) set, like a jewel.

255. *ward:* guard.

259. *shall . . . hire:* shall pay the cost of your efforts. In other words, they will be killed.

263. 'The fact that you have grandchildren when you are old will reward you.'

265. *Advance . . . standards:* raise your banners.

266. *ransom:* penalty.

268. *gain:* profit.

272. Richard and Ratcliff are discussing conversations they have overheard.

God and our good cause fight upon our side;
The prayers of holy saints and wronged souls,
Like high-rear'd bulwarks, stand before our faces;
Richard except, those whom we fight against
Had rather have us win than him they follow.
For what is he they follow? Truly, gentlemen,
A bloody tyrant and a homicide;
One rais'd in blood, and one in blood establish'd;
One that made means to come by what he hath,
And slaughtered those that were the means to help him;
A base foul stone, made precious by the foil
Of England's chair, where he is falsely set;
One that hath ever been God's enemy.
Then if you fight against God's enemy,
God will in justice ward you as his soldiers;
If you do sweat to put a tyrant down,
You sleep in peace, the tyrant being slain;
If you do fight against your country's foes,
Your country's fat shall pay your pains the hire;
If you do fight in safeguard of your wives,
Your wives shall welcome home the conquerors;
If you do free your children from the sword,
Your children's children quits it in your age.
Then, in the name of God and all these rights,
Advance your standards, draw your willing swords.
For me, the ransom of my bold attempt
Shall be this cold corpse on the earth's cold face;
But if I thrive, the gain of my attempt
The least of you shall share his part thereof.
Sound drums and trumpets boldly and cheerfully;
God and Saint George! Richmond and victory!

Exeunt. Re-enter KING RICHARD, RATCLIFF, ATTENDANTS, *and* FORCES

King Richard
What said Northumberland as touching Richmond?

277. Richard is ordering someone to note the time.

279. *the book:* the calendar he is looking at. Remember Richard's first speech in the play: the clouds are louring on the Yorkists once again.
280. *braved:* made it shine splendidly.

290. *vaunts:* rides proudly.

291. *caparison:* cover with a rich cloth.

295. *foreward:* vanguard.
all in length: to its full length.

Ratcliff
That he was never trained up in arms.
King Richard
He said the truth; and what said Surrey then?
Ratcliff
He smil'd, and said 'The better for our purpose'.
King Richard
He was in the right; and so indeed it is.

Clock strikes

Tell the clock there. Give me a calendar.
Who saw the sun to-day?
Ratcliff Not I, my lord.
King Richard
Then he disdains to shine; for by the book
He should have brav'd the east an hour ago.
A black day will it be to somebody.
Ratcliff!
Ratcliff
My lord?
King Richard
The sun will not be seen to-day;
The sky doth frown and lour upon our army.
I would these dewy tears were from the ground.
Not shine to-day! Why, what is that to me
More than to Richmond? For the selfsame heaven
That frowns on me looks sadly upon him.

Enter NORFOLK

Norfolk
Arm, arm, my lord; the foe vaunts in the field.
King Richard
Come, bustle, bustle; caparison my horse;
Call up Lord Stanley, bid him bring his power.
I will lead forth my soldiers to the plain,
And thus my battle shall be ordered:
My foreward shall be drawn out all in length,

296. *foot:* infantrymen.

301. *puissance:* armed force.

302. *winged:* supported on the flanks.

303. *This . . . boot!* Richard feels confident now, that with this plan of battle, and Saint George, the patron saint of England, fighting for them, they have a good chance of winning.

306. *Jockey:* another form of the name Jack or John; as *Dickon* was a form of Dick or Richard.

307. *bought and sold:* betrayed.

308. The rhyme would be intended to lower morale in Richard's army.

310-15. This encouragement by Richard is probably spoken mainly to himself, and shows him still fighting against his despair. The rhyme seems to have spurred him into action.

316-41. The moral level of this speech is far below that of Richmond's address. Which do you think the more realistic, the one likely to make the army fight well?

317. *to cope withal:* to come to grips with.

318. *sort:* gang. He is here speaking of his subjects who have turned against him.

319. *lackey peasants:* hangers-on to the army.

320. *o'er-cloyed:* sick from too much eating; but here it stands for 'over-populated'.

324. *restrain:* steal.
distain: dishonour.

Consisting equally of horse and foot;
Our archers shall be placed in the midst.
John Duke of Norfolk, Thomas Earl of Surrey,
Shall have the leading of this foot and horse.
They thus directed, we will follow
In the main battle, whose puissance on either side
Shall be well winged with our chiefest horse.
This, and Saint George to boot! What think'st thou,
Norfolk?

Norfolk

A good direction, warlike sovereign.
This found I on my tent this morning.

He sheweth him a paper

King Richard [*Reads*]

'Jockey of Norfolk, be not so bold,
For Dickon thy master is bought and sold.'
A thing devised by the enemy.
Go, gentlemen, every man unto his charge.
Let not our babbling dreams affright our souls;
Conscience is but a word that cowards use,
Devis'd at first to keep the strong in awe.
Our strong arms be our conscience, swords our law.
March on, join bravely, let us to it pell-mell;
If not to heaven, then hand in hand to hell.

His Oration to his Army

What shall I say more than I have inferr'd?
Remember whom you are to cope withal—
A sort of vagabonds, rascals, and runaways,
A scum of Britaines, and base lackey peasants,
Whom their o'er-cloyed country vomits forth
To desperate adventures and assur'd destruction.
You sleeping safe, they bring to you unrest;
You having lands, and bless'd with beauteous wives,
They would restrain the one, distain the other.
And who doth lead them but a paltry fellow,

326. *mother's cost:* In fact, Richard's brother-in-law, the Duke of Burgundy, had supported Richmond.

329. *whip:* Tramps and vagabonds were whipped out of towns in Shakespeare's England.
330. *over-weening:* proud.

332. 'Who if they had not had this crazy adventure to dream about, ...'
333. *For . . . means:* because they were so poor.

336. *bobb'd:* hit with their fists. Richard's words here make them seem feeble opponents whom a good clout can keep in order.

343. *welkin:* the sky overhead. Richard thinks of his men as riding so hard into the fight that their lances will, on impact, shatter and be flung high in the air.

347. *is pass'd the marsh:* Richmond had moved into a good tactical position, and had therefore to be fought with immediately.

349. Now that the battle is about to start, Richard is full of courage.

352. *spleen:* fierce temper.

Long kept in Britaine at our mother's cost?
A milk-sop, one that never in his life
Felt so much cold as over shoes in snow?
Let's whip these stragglers o'er the seas again;
Lash hence these over-weening rags of France,
These famish'd beggars, weary of their lives;
Who, but for dreaming on this fond exploit,
For want of means, poor rats, had hang'd themselves.
If we be conquered, let men conquer us,
And not these bastard Britaines, whom our fathers
Have in their own land beaten, bobb'd, and thump'd,
And, in record, left them the heirs of shame.
Shall these enjoy our lands? lie with our wives,
Ravish our daughters? [*Drum afar off*] Hark! I hear their drum.
Fight, gentlemen of England! Fight, bold yeomen!
Draw, archers, draw your arrows to the head!
Spur your proud horses hard, and ride in blood;
Amaze the welkin with your broken staves!

Enter a MESSENGER

What says Lord Stanley? Will he bring his power?

Messenger
My lord, he doth deny to come.

King Richard
Off with his son George's head!

Norfolk
My lord, the enemy is pass'd the marsh.
After the battle let George Stanley die.

King Richard
A thousand hearts are great within my bosom.
Advance our standards, set upon our foes;
Our ancient word of courage, fair Saint George,
Inspire us with the spleen of fiery dragons!
Upon them! Victory sits on our helms.

Exeunt

SCENE IV

Stage Direction. *Excursions:* soldiers fighting, moving across the stage

3. 'Wherever there is a dangerous threat, Richard is there to meet it

7-13. Richard's last appearance shows him displaying a virtue—courag —unblemished by his past actions.
7. Richard probably means exactly what he says. A horse was essenti to a general if he was to fight and lead his men successfully, ar fighting well and so restoring his personal honour is now probab much more important than keeping his kingdom.
9. 'I have bet my life on the throw of a dice.' In other words, 'Th battle is a gamble'.
10. *the hazard . . . die:* the luck of the dice.
11. It was a usual trick for several men to wear armour like the leader's, so that the leader himself would be in less danger in the battl Shakespeare refers to it again in *Henry IV Part* 1, when several m are reported to have worn armour like the king's at the battle Shrewsbury.

SCENE V

Richmond enters to meet Richard at the end of Scene iv.

CENE IV—*Another part of the field*

Alarum; excursions. Enter NORFOLK *and* FORCES; *to him* CATESBY

'atesby
Rescue, my Lord of Norfolk, rescue, rescue!
The King enacts more wonders than a man,
Daring an opposite to every danger.
His horse is slain, and all on foot he fights,
Seeking for Richmond in the throat of death.
Rescue, fair lord, or else the day is lost.

Alarums. Enter KING RICHARD

ing Richard
A horse! a horse! my kingdom for a horse!
atesby
Withdraw, my lord; I'll help you to a horse.
ing Richard
Slave, I have set my life upon a cast
And I will stand the hazard of the die.
I think there be six Richmonds in the field;
Five have I slain to-day instead of him.
A horse! a horse! my kingdom for a horse!

Exeunt

NE V—*Another part of the field*

Alarum. Enter RICHARD *and* RICHMOND; *they fight;* RICHARD *is slain. Retreat and Flourish. Enter* RICHMOND, DERBY *bearing the crown, with other* LORDS

hmond
God and your arms be prais'd, victorious friends;
'he day is ours, the bloody dog is dead.

4. *long-usurped royalty:* the crown.

8. To say 'Amen' is to pray that something will happen.

15. *Inter:* bury.

18. *as . . . sacrament:* sworn before God, at Mass.

19. The white rose is the symbol of the house of York, and the r rose, of the house of Lancaster. Richmond, a Lancastrian, will un them by marrying Elizabeth, daughter of Edward IV, a Yorkist.

22. He means that anyone who does not wish the marriage to ta place must be considered a traitor.

24-6. Richmond is looking back to the whole period of the civil wa the Wars of the Roses.

26. *compell'd:* forced into one of the armies.
27-31. 'Let Richmond and Elizabeth now join together, according God's law, all those things that York and Lancaster previou divided.'
30. *true succeeders:* rightful heirs.
31. *ordinance:* law.
32. *their heirs:* Queen Elizabeth I, the queen of England at the ti when the play was written, was, of course, the grand-daughter Richmond, now King Henry VII. There is a touch of flattery here
33. *smooth-fac'd:* not frowning. Remember Richard's first spee 'Grim-visag'd war hath smooth'd his wrinkl'd front'.

Derby

Courageous Richmond, well hast thou acquit thee!
Lo, here, this long-usurped royalty
From the dead temples of this bloody wretch
Have I pluck'd off, to grace thy brows withal.
Wear it, enjoy it, and make much of it.

Richmond

Great God of heaven, say Amen to all!
But, tell me is young George Stanley living.

Derby

He is, my lord, and safe in Leicester town,
Whither, if it please you, we may now withdraw us.

Richmond

What men of name are slain on either side?

Derby

John Duke of Norfolk, Walter Lord Ferrers,
Sir Robert Brakenbury, and Sir William Brandon.

Richmond

Inter their bodies as becomes their births.
Proclaim a pardon to the soldiers fled
That in submission will return to us.
And then, as we have ta'en the sacrament,
We will unite the white rose and the red.
Smile heaven upon this fair conjunction,
That long have frown'd upon their enmity!
What traitor hears me, and says not amen?
England hath long been mad, and scarr'd herself;
The brother blindly shed the brother's blood,
The father rashly slaughter'd his own son,
The son, compell'd, been butcher to the sire;
All this divided York and Lancaster,
Divided in their dire division,
O, now let Richmond and Elizabeth,
The true succeeders of each royal house,
By God's fair ordinance conjoin together!
And let their heirs, God, if thy will be so,
Enrich the time to come with smooth-fac'd peace,

35. *Abate:* blunt.
36. *reduce:* bring back.

38. *increase:* prosperity.

With smiling plenty, and fair prosperous days!
Abate the edge of traitors, gracious Lord,
That would reduce these bloody days again
And make poor England weep in streams of blood!
Let them not live to taste this land's increase
That would with treason wound this fair land's peace!
Now civil wounds are stopp'd, peace lives again—
That she may long live here, God say amen!

Exeunt

SUMMING UP

The central figure

In the Introduction it was suggested that Richard's part in the play is an overwhelmingly important one, and that what has always fascinated people about him is his wickedness. Now that you have read the play it is appropriate to examine Richard's character more closely. There is a peculiar quality about his wickedness which one can only call 'joyful', and it is exercised in a remarkable variety of roles: ruthless plotter, successful lover, king, war-leader and, on many occasions, accomplished actor. Although he complains bitterly that he has not had a fair chance in life because of his deformity, his energy and ingenuity are the things that seem most impressive about him. His twisted body may give him the excuse for being *subtle, false and treacherous*, but this quickly falls into the background as we watch his sheer talent in action in pursuit of an evil ambition.

The zestful quality of Richard's wickedness is well illustrated in his encounter with Anne in Act I, Scene ii. She blames Richard for the deaths of her husband and of her father-in-law, whose body she is accompanying. She curses him elaborately, demanding particularly that any wife he may marry should:

> *be made*
> *More miserable by the death of him*
> *Than I am made by my young lord and thee!*
> (Act I, Scene ii, lines 26-8)

Promptly Richard appears, like a devil perversely responding to the curse, and, within minutes, he is thoroughly enjoying himself pretending to woo her, addressing her as *divine perfection of a woman*, and *Fairer than tongue can name thee*. The two of them play an elaborate word game something like the savage ritual of two animals about to mate, and eventually Anne gives way, underlining in the process the potential terrible irony of her curse on Richard's future wife. Richard's triumphant speech at the end of the scene is worth close examination, with its grim humour, frank self-knowledge and, finally, a kind of ironic delight in his own ugliness:

Shine out, fair sun, till I have bought a glass,
That I may see my shadow as I pass.
(Act I, Scene ii, lines 262-3)

If one's first reaction to Richard is horror and revulsion, these feelings must soon be replaced by a sort of guilty delight, especially when the villain appeals directly to his audience (as he does in this speech) in the manner favoured by the Elizabethan theatre. (Marlowe's Barabas in *The Jew of Malta* and Shakespeare's Edmund in *King Lear* are other examples of this technique.) Superman, challenging man and God and getting his own way, can hardly fail to appeal to one side of human nature. And the more atrocious Richard's behaviour becomes, somehow the more fascinating he is—up to a point. The whole-heartedness of the acting out of his chosen role is shown on many occasions. When he says to King Edward:

. . . if any here,
Hold me a foe—
. . . I desire
To reconcile me to his friendly peace:
'Tis death to me to be at enmity;
I hate it, and desire all good men's love.
(Act II, Scene i, lines 54-62)

it is almost impossible not to laugh out loud. There is a typically crazy, but dangerous, humour about him in Act III, Scene vii, when he appears *aloft, between two bishops* in an elaborate trick to persuade the Lord Mayor and citizens of London to support his claim to the throne. His show of reluctance to take power, and Buckingham's feverish efforts to squeeze some sign of enthusiasm out of the suspicious citizens, verge on pantomime, but the sheer outrageousness of Richard's hypocritical acceptance holds the stage:

Since you will buckle fortune on my back,
To bear her burden, whe'er I will or no,
I must have patience to endure the load;
(Act III, Scene vii, lines 227-9)

Many of us probably have dreams or entertain fantasies at times in which we act with utter irresponsibility: for most people complete abandonment of moral restraints has its attraction, even if they rarely succumb to it. Perhaps this is what makes Richard such a fascinating theatrical figure. We can sit for a while in the theatre, secretly identifying ourselves with him, before we go back to our normal routine lives, leaving the warped glamour of a savage time behind.

When we return from such fantasies to the real world, we usually recognize them as impracticable and undesirable. We only have to think of the twisted dictators of our own century, the way they rose to power, to see that behaviour like Richard's cannot really be tolerated in a healthy society. So Shakespeare couldn't leave us with a rampant, triumphant Richard. Many dictators overstep the mark at some stage in their careers, outraging their subjects or their enemies to the point of desperate retaliation. Richard's fortunes begin to change at the beginning of Act IV, and the turning point is the murder of the Princes in the Tower, a crime which seems to us, and to Shakespeare too, distinctly more horrible than anything else Richard does. After all, most of his other victims are not only adults, but are themselves ambitious, predatory characters in a world where only the ruthless survive. In Act IV, Scene ii he said to the (for once) squeamish Buckingham:

I wish the bastards dead.
And I would have it suddenly perform'd.
(Act IV, Scene ii, lines 18-19)

and from now on Shakespeare leaves us in no doubt that Richard is on the downward path. Even before this, opposition had been developing, but it is the attitude of Richard himself that shows significant change. The zest, the sense of delight in playing his role, falters, and he begins to lose control of affairs. In Act IV, Scene iv, news comes of rebellions in several parts of the country, to add to the opposition of Richmond, Dorset, Buckingham, Derby, and his mother, the Duchess of York. His confidence becomes erratic, and even words fail him when his mother confronts him with some 'home truths':

No, by the holy rood, thou know'st it well
Thou cam'st on earth to make the earth my hell.
(Act IV, Scene iv, lines 166-7)

He can reply only with a particularly feeble pun. In Act V

his confidence disintegrates completely: ghosts distract him in his dreams, and when Ratcliffe comes to rouse him for the battle his fearfulness is almost pathetic. He even uses religious language seriously (*Have mercy, Jesu!* and *By the apostle Paul*) and considers the weather omens with nervous intensity:

The sun will not be seen today;
The sky doth frown and lour upon our army.
(Act V, Scene iii, lines 284-5)

If it is true that one tends to identify with the confident illain in the first half of the play, how does one react to he irritable, frightened criminal of the second half? For nany observers the change probably corresponds with the eturn from fantasy mentioned above. For a while audiences nay be swept away on the tide of arrogant vitality, respond-ng with a chuckle, or a grunt of admiring astonishment, out they know that this sort of thing cannot be allowed to o on indefinitely. Sooner or later self-indulgence and con-empt for others' feelings—in ourselves as well as in Richard —must be put in their place. As we leave the theatre and eturn to daily life we accept Richard's decline and fall as, oughly, just and inevitable. There is a great deal here that s obviously relevant to our lives today. Whether human ature changes or not, there can be few of those who watch *Richard III* in the theatre, or even read it in the schoolroom, ho do not feel the attraction of the ascendant Richard and et recognize the rightness of his final defeat and destruc-on. For, fascinating as it may be, utter self-centredness is ltimately horrific, and most of us know it.

ome major themes and their effects

ertain aspects of the play, collected under the rough title hemes', are briefly presented in the Index at the end of this ook. But there are two or three pervading themes which o much to hold the play together, to give it dramatic hape and impact, which should be discussed at rather reater length here.

Little has been said, so far, about God in the play, except at Richard amuses himself, early on, with flippant ferences to religion, and later, facing death, is forced to ke it more seriously. But there is hardly a page on which

God, damnation and redemption are not in some way mentioned. Many of the references are very elaborate. When the two murderers go to the Tower to kill Clarence they have a long theological discussion with him and he appeals movingly to them to spare him on religious grounds. There are also innumerable references to devils (Richard is frequently described as a fiend or a devil), many images of Heaven and Hell, and many curses. Those who have seen the play performed will have noticed a remarkable number of clergymen on the stage. Apart from the two Archbishops, the Bishop of Ely, 'Christopher Urswick, a Priest' and 'John, another Priest', who all appear in the list of characters, many other churchmen put in an appearance—at the funeral procession of Henry VI, when Richard ascends the throne, and on the occasions when people are executed.

All this, and much more, implies, as the play proceeds, that Richard's true adversary is God himself, and that, however contemptuous he may be, however carelessly he throws away religious terms, he will eventually be brought to book. The main channel of communication with God throughout is the human conscience, and there are many instances of its workings, the most striking ones, perhaps, being Clarence's frightful dream (Act I, Scene iv, lines 1-74), King Edward's remorse about Clarence's death (Act II, Scene i, lines 104-35) and, finally, Richard's fearful rousing from his dream (Act V, Scene iii, lines 178-207).

The dramatic force of religion in the play is emphasized by the deceptiveness of appearances. With Richard, in the earlier scenes, we may well share a cynical outlook on the Church and the place of religion in society. Anne's pious rage, for example, quickly gives way to an odd kind of fascination with the persuasive Richard and, in the process she deceives herself in religious terms:

. . . much it joys me too
To see you are become so penitent.
(Act I, Scene ii, lines 219-20)

Clarence is as much deceived as anyone, and has to be brutally enlightened by one of his murderers (*You are deceiv'd: your brother Gloucester hates you:* Act I, Scene iv line 225) as he faces divine retribution at death. In Act III Scene iv, the Bishop of Ely, deceived (or self-deceiving bustles off to fetch strawberries to keep Richard happy. There are many instances of such deception and self-deception, leading to the last two Acts, by which stage hardly anyone can remain deceived, however much he wants to. As the deceptions dissolve, God moves to assert himself in human society through the agency of Richmond, who sees himself as leading God's army against Richard:

O Thou, whose captain I account myself,
Look on my forces with a gracious eye;
(Act V, Scene iii, lines 109-10)

at the same time that Richard is facing the reality of his crimes as the ghosts of his victims visit him in sleep. The ghosts themselves in turn curse Richard and bless Richmond. In the end God is not mocked.

These main themes are conveyed and supported by Shakespeare's choice of language and imagery in a remarkably consistent manner. In this *Richard III* shows a great advance on the previous Histories, the three parts of *Henry VI.* The religious terminology has already been mentioned, but another striking feature of the play is the animal imagery applied to Richard himself. He is compared with a savage dog several times:

That dog, that had his teeth before his eyes
To worry lambs and lap their gentle blood . . .
(Act IV, Scene iv, lines 49-50)

and also with a toad, a *bottled spider*, a hedgehog, a *rooting hog* and a boar. The effect of all these comparisons is to accentuate his ferocity and ugliness and, finally, to make him seem a creature fit only for destruction by an avenging God.

The play as history

Shakespeare's interest in history was, it seems, a qualified one. Like many Elizabethans he was acutely aware of England's increasing importance in the world, and at various stages in his career he examined much of the preceding two centuries, tracing the complicated historical process which produced Queen Elizabeth, the Gloriana of the poets, the celebrated Virgin Queen. His first attempt of this kind was in three parts of *Henry VI*, followed by *Richard III.* In writing the latter play Shakespeare relied on the chronicles of Holinshed and Hall: these were subjective and often inaccurate registers of events, and Shakespeare certainly didn't feel bound to adhere strictly even to these. For his job was that of dramatic poet first and foremost, reserving the right to pursue truth in his own way—the truth of human nature, of man in society and of the effect of power on political individuals. It is easy to show that *Richard III* is in many respects historically inaccurate: some modern historians, with more information at their command than Hall, Holinshed or Shakespeare, say that Richard greatly admired his brother, Edward IV; that he was happily married; that he was greatly respected, even loved, by the North Country people over whom he ruled on his brother's behalf; there is no hard evidence to implicate him in the murder of his nephews, the 'Princes in the Tower'. But when all this is said, it can be seen how relatively unimportant it is, except for those who wish to examine the creative process by which Shakespeare adapted the material available to him and made it into the play we have before us. For most other people 'Shakespeare's Richard' himself is a sufficiently absorbing and profitable study.

THEME INDEX

Kingship
The relation of the man to the office: III vii 155–65
Burdens and care of office: I iii 107–9; III vii 145; IV iv 244–5
Kingly qualities and their opposites: I ii 244; III vii 71–6
A king's effect on his country: II iii 11; III iv 102–4; III vii 124–8; V iii 12–13; V v 23–34

Fulfilment of prophecies and curses
God the avenger and punisher: I ii 62–5, 102–3; I iii 135–6, 180–1, 272–3, 284–7, 303–4; I iv 57, 69–71, 110–11, 185–7, 191–5, 202–3, 212–16; II i 13–15, 34–5, 82; II iii 25–6, 36, 45; III iv 18–21; IV iv 22–4, 55–8, 73–8, 183–4, 378–81; V i 18–24; V ii 22; V iii 114–15, 176–7, 253–4; V v 8, 31–41.
Margaret's curse: I iii 196–232; II ii; III iii 15; III iv 91–2; IV iii; IV iv 79–81.
Other foretellings: I iii 290–302; III ii 67–6; III iv 80; I ii 14–25; 26–8; IV i 65–86; I ii 62–3; II i 32–5; V i 13–17.

Richard scourge and victim
Richard the destroyer: I iii 12–15; I iv 11–20, 113–27, 222–41, 273–5; II ii 20–32; II iii 27; II iv 12–30, 42; III ii 39–55; III iv 7–20; IV i 32; IV iv; V ii 5–13; V iii 243–52; V iv 2–5.
Richard's victims
Clarence: I i 34–40, 117–20, 129–31, 145–50; I iii 73, 84–6, 214–15, 247–50; II i 77–135; II ii 1–15, 72–84; III i 144–5; IV iv 46, 67, 282.
Hastings: I i 68–9, 73–7; I iii 89–90; III i 161–93; II vi; IV i 121; IV iv 148; V i 3.
The young princes: II ii 121–2, 145–9; II iv 1; III v 108–9; IV i 4–23, 99–104; IV ii 10–82; IV iv.
Buckingham: I iii 288-302; II i 32-40; III i 1-95, 132-200; III v; IV iii 47 50; IV iv 439, 468, 507–17, 533–40.
Anne: I ii 153–9; IV ii 51–9; IV ii 39; IV iv 283.
Elizabeth: I i 64–110; I iii 27, 152–3; III iv 72; III vii 184–91.
Margaret: I iii 110–43, 215–39; IV iv 1-125.
6–94.

Richmond God's agent
V i 44, 50; IV ii 49, 89–111; IV iii 40–1, 46; IV iv 437, 463–499, 524–9, 534–6; IV v; V iii 219, 271–2; V iv 5, 11.

FURTHER READING

Shakespeare's chief source for the Richard he presents was Holinshed's Chronicles. A modern edition of the relevant parts can be found in *Shakespeare's Holinshed* (Everyman Library: Dent).

A modern biography and interpretation of Richard's life and reign that presents him in a much more favourable light than either Holinshed or Shakespeare is *Richard III* by P. M. Kendall (Allen and Unwin).

E. M. W. Tillyard's *Shakespeare's History Plays* (Peregrine Books) relates the Histories to their sources and to other treatments of the historical subjects in Elizabethan times, and offers an interpretation of the Histories related to each other that has been widely accepted.

In *The Villain as Hero in Elizabethan Tragedy* (Routledge and Kegan Paul), C. V. Boyer compares Richard with other dramatic villains of the period, and relates them to the convention of which they form a part.

John Palmer's *Political Characters of Shakespeare* (Macmillan) deals with Richard and other Shakespearian figures such as Brutus, Henry V and Coriolanus, and shows their common characteristics as leaders and politicians.

There are interesting chapters on *Richard III* in the following books:

I. Ribner, *The English History Play in the Age of Shakespeare* (Methuen);

M. M. Reese, *The Cease of Majesty, a Study of Shakespeare's History Plays* (Arnold);

H. Craig, *An Interpretation of Shakespeare* (Dryden Press of New York).

Those who develop a deep interest in the play will want to read W. H. Clemen's *A Commentary on Shakespeare's 'Richard III'* (Methuen), a full-scale, scholarly study of the play. Keeping in mind that it is Shakespeare's presentation of the character of Richard which is important to a student of literature regardless of its historical validity, others might enjoy the modern, semi-fictional reconstruction of the period in Josephine Tey's *The Daughter of Time* (Penguin).